Project Analysis for Local Development

Westview Special Studies

The concept of Westview Special Studies is a response to the continuing crisis in academic and informational publishing. Library budgets are being diverted from the purchase of books and used for data banks, computers, micromedia, and other methods of information retrieval. Interlibrary loan structures further reduce the edition sizes required to satisfy the needs of the scholarly community. Economic pressures on university presses and the few private scholarly publishing companies have greatly limited the capacity of the industry to properly serve the academic and research communities. As a result, many manuscripts dealing with important subjects, often representing the highest level of scholarship, are no longer economically viable publishing projects--or, if accepted for publication, are typically subject to lead times ranging from one to three years.

Westview Special Studies are our practical solution to the problem. As always, the selection criteria include the importance of the subject, the work's contribution to scholarship, and its insight, originality of thought, and excellence of exposition. We accept manuscripts in camera-ready form, typed, set, or word processed according to specifications laid out in our comprehensive manual, which contains straightforward instructions and sample pages. The responsibility for editing and proofreading lies with the author or sponsoring institution, but our editorial staff is always available to answer questions and provide guidance.

The result is a book printed on acid-free paper and bound in sturdy library-quality soft covers. We manufacture these books ourselves using equipment that does not require a lengthy make-ready process and that allows us to publish first editions of 300 to 1000 copies and to reprint even smaller quantities as needed. Thus, we can produce Special Studies quickly and can keep even very specialized books in print as long as there is a demand for them.

About the Book and Author

The increasing importance of local-level planning in developing countries and disillusionment with highly theoretical, sophisticated methodologies have prompted the creation of this simple-to-use manual for planners and administrators seeking to identify, evaluate, and select local-level development projects. This book outlines information required for thorough project evaluation, sources of that information (including alternative approaches to data collection), methods of analysis (with detailed explanations of their strengths and weaknesses), and techniques for organizing the results for purposes of decision making. Unlike many abstract procedural guides for development that require substantial data and technical manpower --two resources usually unavailable at local levels--this book is meant for planners and administrators who have had little or no formal training in project analysis and planning. Mr. Mathur supplements his step-by-step methodology with explanations of how and when to make appropriate and effective use of the techniques.

Om Prakash Mathur is director of the National Institute of Urban Affairs, New Delhi, and a former staff member of the United Nations Centre for Regional Development.

Published in cooperation with the
United Nations Centre for Regional Development

Project Analysis for Local Development

Om Prakash Mathur

Routledge
Taylor & Francis Group
NEW YORK AND LONDON

To

COLIN BRUCE, AVROM BENDAVID-VAL, ERIC CHETWYND,
JIM GOATERS, H.M. GUNASEKERA, BENJAMIN HIGGINS,
BRUNO KNALL, R.P. MISRA, ANDERS RICHTERS,
DENNIS RONDINELLI, HIDEHIKO SAZANAMI, MASAFUMI
TANIFUJI, SUMIKO TORII, and to TOSHIHIRO YOGO

I am grateful to them for making this book possible.

First published in paperback 2024

First published 1985 by Westview Press, Inc.

Published 2019 by Routledge
605 Third Avenue, New York, NY 10158

and by Routledge
4 Park Square, Milton Park, Abingdon, Oxon OX14 4RN

Routledge is an imprint of the Taylor & Francis Group, an informa business

Library of Congress Catalog Card Number: 85-13797

Publisher's Note
The publisher has gone to great lengths to ensure the quality of this reprint but points out that some imperfections in the original copies may be apparent.

ISBN 13: 978-0-367-28444-2 (hbk)
ISBN 13: 978-0-367-29990-3 (pbk)
ISBN 13: 978-0-429-30319-7 (ebk)

DOI: 10.4324/9780429303197

Contents

Tables, Figures Examples, and Formats

TABLES

FIGURES

EXAMPLES

FORMATS

Preface

This book has a short history, which I would like to share with its readers. The history goes back to the year 1981 when my colleagues and myself at the United Nations Centre for Regional Development (Nagoyá, Japan) were engaged in pretesting the drafts of training modules on local-level planning that we had prepared in response to a request from the Government of Bangladesh/UNICEF, Dhaka. During the pretest session on how to analyze and appraise local-level development projects for which I was responsible, the participants, which included the Upa-Zilla level (a lower-level administrative unit in Bangladesh) functionaries, the elected representatives, and the faculty members of the Rural Development Academy (Bogra, Bangladesh), gave scores of examples to show that in actual practice people in the position of decision making hardly ever attempt to systematically analyze development projects. The entire process of project selection is woefully ad hoc and is influenced by decision maker's predilections. Almost universally the participants considered project-planning exercises superfluous and sterile. On my part, I used their examples to demonstrate that the inadequacies in the existing practices lay not as much with the selection process as with the objectives of decision makers in making the selection. If the objectives of decision makers were antidevelopmental, as indeed these were in the examples given by the participants, then, I argued, these would be reflected in the selection process. At the end of the pretest dialogue that lasted four days, I succeeded--at least I believe so--in drawing a distinction between the process of identifying the benefits and costs of candidate projects, and the objectives and motives that underlie the selection process. I also succeeded in convincing them that project analysis was not such a dreadful exercise as they thought, and what they had to do was to translate the objectives and goals of local-level planning into specific selection criteria and to use the criteria for evaluation of candidate projects. A somewhat exacting process but not out of bounds for functionaries even at local levels!

Upon my return to the United Nations Centre for Regional Development from the Rural Development Academy, Bogra, where the pretest sessions were held, I was struck for the first time by the absence of a publication that would explain to planners and administrators of relatively small administrative units the entire process of arriving at decisions on development projects as well as the rationale of the process. My original draft on the subject was grossly inadequate, and even if it was rearranged and padded with fresh examples from the field, I did not think it would serve the overall purpose of strengthening local-level planning practices. Why not attempt a book, I asked. There were heavy risks, as a very large number of books, manuals, and guidelines already existed on the subject. The World Bank, UNIDO, ESCAP, OECD, and many other international and bilateral agencies had invested large sums of money to evolve, refine, and strengthen the methodology for project analysis and planning. Would my book be read or even reach potential markets in the face of the stiff competition? I went over the existing publications on the subject once again and found that in order to be able to use them, the users would necessarily require training in project analysis, an exposure to calculus, and access to large quantities of data. At local levels in developing countries, there was neither the trained manpower nor the quantities of data required for purposes of project analysis. My book found a place and I proceeded to write one. I used earlier versions of the book in training courses for local development officers held in 1982 and 1983 at the Central Panchayat Training Institute (Kathmandu, Nepal), and for the planning officers of the island countries of the Pacific held in 1983 at Honiara, the beautiful capital of the Solomon Islands. Just before resigning my long tenure with the United Nations (Department of Technical Cooperation and Development) in September 1984, I finalized the manuscript and submitted it for publication. I am grateful to Westview Press for accepting it.

The main theme that runs through the book is how to identify, evaluate, and select relatively small-scale development projects. The book does not offer any new or innovative methodology for evaluating these projects; what it does is to make a simple, easily understandable presentation of project evaluation methods already available in the existing literature, and to supplement it with explanations on how and when to use them.

It is designed to enhance the capacity of planners and administrators at local levels and to enable them to do their planning tasks better. It addresses questions such as: What information should the planners collect for identification of projects? From whom should they collect it? How should they analyze and organize that information? What kinds of tools should they use for analysis? Examples, case studies, and readings have been added to the text of the six chapters into which this book is divided. A few exercises have also been included to give practice to those who wish to use the book for self-teaching.

I have separately acknowledged the contributions of those who have helped me, directly or indirectly, in writing this book. I would, however, like to especially acknowledge the contributions of three individuals--namely, Professor Masahiko Honjo, former Director of the United Nations Centre for Regional Development, who inspired me to undertake this venture; Mr. Masafumi Tanifuji, Research Associate; and Ms. Sumiko Torii, Secretary, who provided the day-to-day assistance. I am grateful to each one of them.

Om Prakash Mathur

Project Analysis for Local Development

1
Introduction to Project Planning: Its Context, Definitions, and Stages

WHY IS PROJECT PLANNING IMPORTANT? THE CONTEXT OF PROJECT PLANNING

One of the very complex problems with which we, as planners and administrators in the developing countries, are currently faced is how to plan, prepare, and select projects that will help in accomplishing the various development goals and objectives. The concern for improved project planning--this phrase being used generically to include various project planning stages[1]--has assumed a new urgency in most developing countries. Three decades of planning and development efforts have not been able to bring about any noticeable improvement in the living conditions of the people. Poverty, unemployment, rising disparities of various sorts, economic and social divisiveness, marginalization of various sections of the population, and a deteriorating quality of life can be seen spreading their tentacles in most parts of the developing world. Little change is reported to have taken place in the consumption standards of the people living in the developing countries. Nearly 750 million people, or 33 percent of the total population in developing countries (excluding China), are said to be living in absolute poverty.[2] One has only to glance at the numerous reports of the World Bank, the United Nations, and the plan documents of the developing countries to see how large the gap between the dreams of the planners and ground realities has grown in recent years. In countries such as Bangladesh, the incidence of poverty has engulfed over 80 percent of the population, who live in a state of acute malnutrition, illiteracy and unemployment.[3]

Surely, all the blame for this state of conditions cannot be placed on poor or faulty project planning practices and procedures. The causes are many and complex, and in several cases attributable to the unjust, inequitable, and exploitative international, national, and regional systems. At the same time, there is no doubt that the absence of systematic identification and formulation of projects is the single most important reason for "failure" on the development front. There is a growing feeling, not altogether unsubstantiated by facts from the field, that the right kinds of projects are just not chosen, and those who are responsible for project identification and formulation pay scant attention to evaluating whether the proposed projects will contribute to the various development objectives or not. Evaluation of the likely impact of the proposed projects on societal growth and development is also not carried out in a befitting manner.

J. Price Gittinger, one of the authorities on the subject, notes that many of the problems of implementation of development programs can be traced to poor project preparation, and writes that:

> Administrators, even those in important planning positions, continually underestimate the time and effort needed to prepare suitable projects. So much attention is paid to policy formulation and planning of a much broader scope that administrators often overlook the specific projects on which to spend the available money and on which much development depends. Ill-conceived, hastily planned projects, virtually improvised on the spot, are too often the result.[4]

These remarks can hardly be considered as exaggerated. Most people in the developing countries are aware of the fact that only in a few cases, and those cases would represent projects of strategic importance to the country's economy, is a proper analysis of alternative project proposals carried out. Proposals for most other types of projects are accepted or rejected without being subjected to any critical scrutiny. The whole process is marked by a high degree of *ad hocism*.

At subnational, local levels such as the Upa-Zillas in Bangladesh, Blocks in India, Districts in Kenya, Kabupatens in Indonesia, and Municipios in Colombia and Mexico, the situation with respect to planning of projects is more disconcerting in the sense that it is not even considered an issue of any importance. Writing in the context of the situation in Bangladesh, A. Abdul Hye, former Director of the Integrated Rural Development Programme in the country wrote:

> The case studies . . . included a few where the local level plans brought frustrating experience instead of desired results. This was due to inadequate attention paid to the analysis of constraints and potentials of particular activities. The selection of appropriate projects is as crucially important in local level plans as elsewhere. The selection should be based on feasibility studies, resource inventories and implementation capacity. In very few cases this was done in the past.[5]

The situation was made worse by the existence in several countries of the view that systematic project analysis involving comparisons of benefits with costs, or even weighing the advantages of one technological mix against another is not necessary for local level development projects. According to the prevalent view, these projects need smaller investments, and, therefore, it is not worthwhile spending much time and energy on examining or evaluating them. It is implied that the main concern of the governments should be to strengthen planning procedures for large-scale projects such as cement plants, fertilizer factories, steel mills, railways, ports, national highways, etc., while local projects such as primary schools, health centers, basic communications, minor irrigation works, small and village industries, and special development schemes for disadvantaged groups of the population can be accepted or rejected without considering, in any appreciable detail "what will projects do, who will benefit from them, are there other projects that can achieve the same objectives with lower costs, etc." Even in countries where procedures for approval of local projects have been laid down, greater emphasis is found to be placed on the "cost" side (how much it will cost, on what items, etc.) rather than the "benefit" side of the project.

This way of thinking and the accompanying arguments are misconceived, to say the least. In countries that are largely rural and where improvement in living conditions is being sought through a set of decentralized, small-scale programs, much greater concerted attention to selection and preparation of projects is necessary. These projects affect the daily lives of the people. Faulty selection of projects or their inadequate preparation can make a world of difference to their existence. Not only this, the effects of such projects can be easily felt at local levels compared to those which involve millions of takas, rupees, or pesos. Who is taking advantage of a minor irrigation project, rich or poor farmers; or who are the main users of a newly paved road, can be easily assessed at these levels. These are significant issues but have nevertheless been grossly ignored by planners in most developing countries.

Most local development plans are in the nature of inventories of resources, and to some extent a cataloging of demands (shopping lists as these are called) of various sorts. The relationship between the two parts, i.e., the resource inventories and the demand for projects, is feeble, to use a rather conservative expression. Quite often, justification for projects is sought on the plea that a particular area has an idle or underutilized resource, and therefore, a project for its use should be taken up. Or, the argument will be given that 60 percent of the farmers in a particular local area do not use a high-yielding variety (HYV) of seeds, and so there should be a project for the introduction of HYV of paddy. Few plans would contain any analysis of why farmers have not been able to adopt high-yielding varieties, let alone recommending a project for farmers to understand the benefits of HYV, and adopt high-yielding seeds in place of traditional ones. There is very little analysis of resources in relation to needs, and how the two can be matched via the selection and promotion of viable projects.

It is within this context that planning for local level projects becomes extremely important. Systematic project planning is vital to economic and social development. Only through concerted attention to the steps involved in planning of projects can the local planners hope to accomplish the objectives laid down in programs such as the Integrated Rural Development Programme in India, the recently initiated Kilusang Kabuhayan at Kaunlaran in the Philippines, or the programs for the economic uplift of small farmers/landless labor underway in many countries. Projects are instruments of change. Selection of the right kind of projects alone can ensure improvement in the living conditions of the poorer sections of the local communities. It is a prerequisite to local development. Dennis Rondinelli's summing up on the importance of project planning is relevant:

> In the framework of planned economic development, the conception, identification and definition of projects and programmes are at the crux of the development process. If theorists are correct in asserting that the essence of development lies in increasing productivity, in promoting structural change to expand the capacity or potential for socioeconomic production, then projects are a critical means of achieving development.[6]

PLANNING FOR PROJECTS: WHAT DO WE UNDERSTAND BY PROJECTS?

It is perhaps useful to begin this section by making a brief reference to the definition of a "project." According to most textbooks, "a project is the smallest unit of activity that can be separately planned, analyzed, and administratively implemented."[7] Gittinger sees this as "a specific activity, with a specific starting point and a specific ending point intended to accomplish specific objectives. . . . It is the smallest operational element prepared and implemented as a separate entity. . . . A project is an undertaking an observer can draw a boundary around--at least a conceptual boundary--and say this is the project."[8] According to Dias and Wickramanayake, when a program is broken down into further manageable units, it becomes a project because "this is where the real action takes place."[9] They illustrate this using Figure 1.

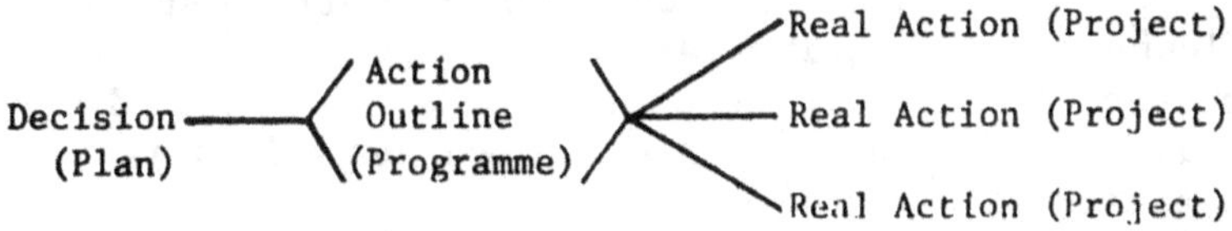

Figure 1. Relationship between plan, programs, and projects

A parallel illustration of the description of a project may also be drawn from the Thana Plan Book of Bangladesh, according to which a plan consists of three plans, namely (1) Drainage and Embankment Plan, (2) Road Plan, and (3) Irrigation Plan. For each of them, there are a number of smaller projects. An approximation is shown in Figure 2.

All these descriptions of a project are related to single investment decisions or activities. The case of Paving the Gravel Road (see Chapter 3) is one such type. In addition, there are projects that are based on integrated approaches. The second case on Integrated Rural Development Project for Gotonia District (IRDPGD) would be the example of a project formulated on the principle of an integrated approach. The essential feature of this kind of project is that it may contain a number of activities that may be related to each other or that may be mutually exclusive. The idea underlying such a project is that the areal/spatial unit for which it may have been designed requires a larger

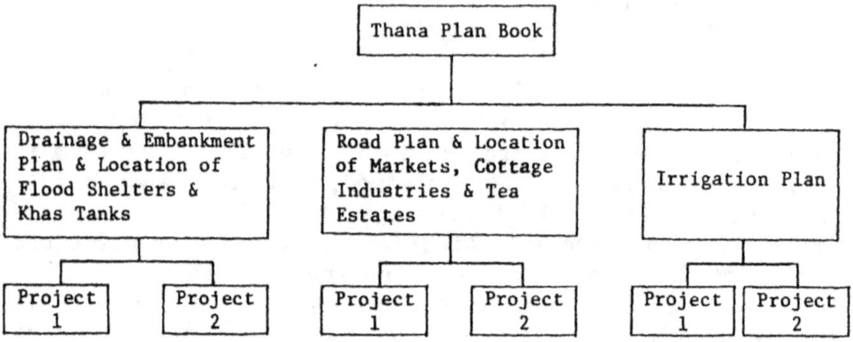

Figure 2. Relationship between plan, programs, and projects

number of activities (agriculture, animal husbandry, irrigation, education, health, nutrition) in order to speed up its development. It requires a simultaneity of actions. There is a specific goal and objective to be accomplished that is possible only by initiating action on several fronts at the same time.

Yet another category would be of projects whose various components/activities are functionally or spatially linked and related. An illustration of a functionally linked project is given in Figure 3. This is the illustration of a project that envisages a change in the cropping pattern of an area--from a mono-crop to a multiple-crop one. The underlying feature of such projects is that they require a large array of linked projects to be conjunctionally planned, without which they may either not be viable, or their impacts may not be felt over the concerned local area. Such projects become efficient only under conditions where a high degree of interdependence pertains.

Projects can also be viewed with respect to their output characteristics. According to this classification, there will be:

1. Projects that are directly productive: Such projects generally belong to agriculture, fisheries, mining, industry, and similar sectors. The key point is that it is possible to have the outputs of such projects measured or valued in money terms.
2. Projects that are indirectly productive: These would be projects in social and economic services such as schools, health centers, sports facilities,

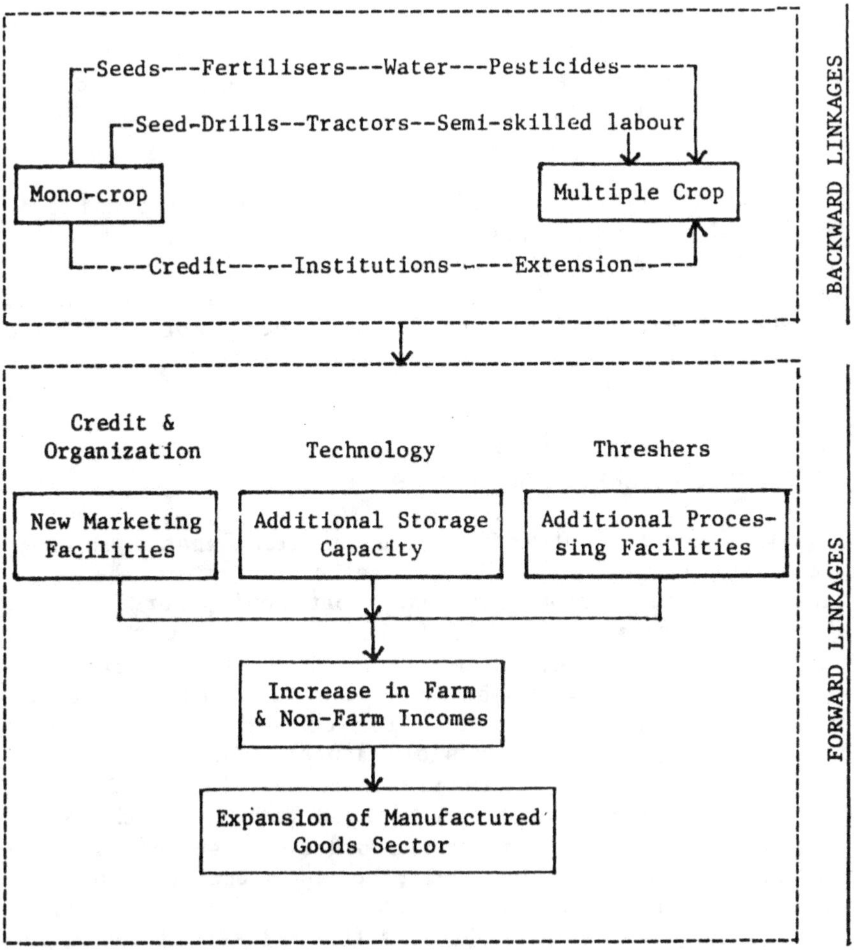

Figure 3. Illustration of a functionally linked project

rural and urban low-cost housing, public utilities such as construction of drains, refuse collection, and in infrastructure sectors such as culverts, roads, bridges, etc. Projects under this group produce services, create conditions that may encourage productive activities, or may improve the general environment of the area. Putting money values on the output of these projects is not possible although some authors and institutions claim to have done it by using proxies or surrogates.

3. Projects that are designed especially for the eco-

nomic and social upliftment of the weaker sections of the society, such as the women, children, and other bypassed groups. This category would also include projects designed especially for the development of backward/depressed areas.

In this book, we shall be concerned with planning of individual projects: how to identify, prepare, and select them. The coverage will extend to all three categories of projects mentioned above. Reference will also be made to the need for packaging and linking them, spatially and functionally.

WHAT DOES PROJECT PLANNING INVOLVE? THE PROJECT PLANNING SEQUENCE

In order to best address the question "what does project planning involve?" a local level situation may be simulated for illustration purposes. What would, for instance, be the main interest of an agricultural officer working in a municipio, a markaz, or a kabupaten? His interest, or rather interests, would be several. He would like to see that the budgetary allocations for the agricultural sector are utilized in the best possible manner. He would want to allocate resources for those projects that, in his view, can contribute most to the objectives and targets of the agricultural sector. His interest would be in selecting projects from a larger pool or shelf; he would therefore want to widen the pool by undertaking surveys and studies of various kinds. He would like to give his fullest attention to the various technical and other details of the projects such as the scale, the number and types of machinery and labor to be employed, the volume of the investments, administrative and supervisory requirements, and so on, so that the projects do not encounter any problems in implementation. He might want to look into the social aspects of the projects. Who will benefit from them? Will the projects create employment in the area? Would they reduce income disparities? Project planning involves all this, and more. It is a tool by which the local level functionaries can identify good projects. It is a mechanism that can enable them to make sound investment decisions. It provides planners at local levels with a methodology of comparing and presenting costs and benefits of alternative project proposals, and assists them in deciding which of the alternatives is the best one.[10]

The tasks of local level planners are, however, not confined to viewing the desirability and viability of projects *per se*. They are also responsible for placing the projects in a wider economic and social perspective. They are concerned with the need for projects--what will be accomplished by them and, equally important, how will the projects fit into the overall program of local development. It means that "project planning" is a part of the larger planning process, and not independent of it. It is important to recognize the inseparability of project planning from the overall planning process, as at times an impression is sought to be created that the search for projects can begin only when a "plan" has been prepared, while at other times it is argued that the plan should be finalized only after projects have been identified and selected. This kind of a discussion--of the chicken first/egg first variety--has done much damage to the development of a comprehensive planning methodology that would embrace both the preparation of a plan as well as the identification of projects. Somehow, the two processes have been dealt with, and continue to be dealt with, separately, often at the cost of each other, although in actual practice the two should be closely intertwined.[11]

Little and Mirrlees have pointed out the necessity of viewing the two processes together in their widely read textbook. They write:

> Good realistic plans can hardly be formulated in the absence of a great deal of project planning, and without proper economic appraisal of projects. This should be obvious: in fact it has been almost everywhere neglected.
>
> But it is also true that the best economic appraisal of projects cannot be made without a plan. To choose the right projects, one must have an estimate of the demand for the product. But how can one estimate the domestic demand for any product unless one has some idea of how the economy will develop. And how the economy develops in turn depends on the long range plans and policies of the government.[12]

Project planning itself has a cycle of its own involving several sequential and iterative steps. It may be mentioned that not all textbooks describe the cycle in exactly the same fashion but both their essence and message remain the same. Guidelines for Rural Centre Planning[13] has identified the following seven steps that constitute the project planning cycle. These are:

1. Project identification and appraisal
2. Prefeasibility studies
3. Feasibility studies
4. Detailed design
5. Project implementation
6. Operation and maintenance
7. Monitoring and evaluation

In Rondinelli's schema, the stages are, in general terms, the same, but he prefers to view project planning as part of the overall cycle that also embraces management. His schema, as given in Project Planning and Implementation in Developing Countries, is shown in Figure 4.[14]

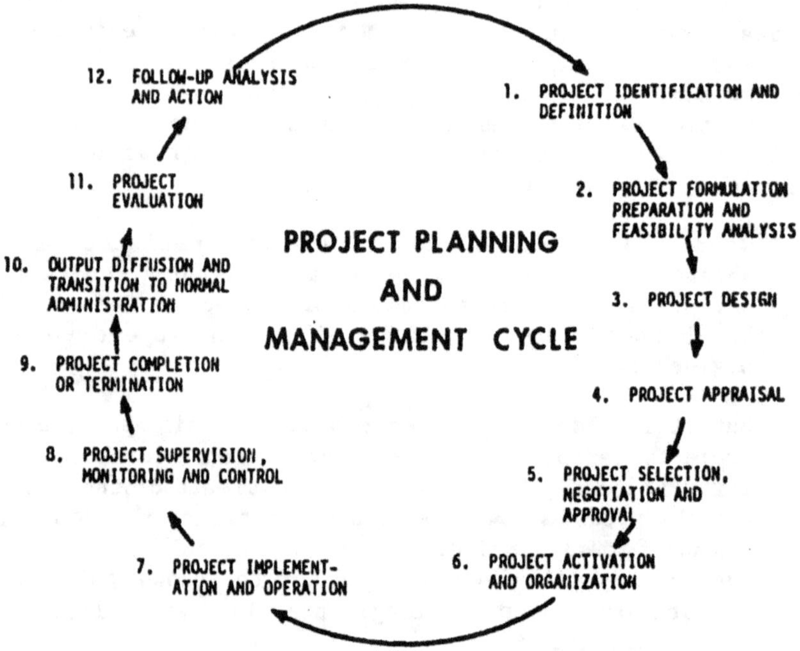

Figure 4. Project planning and management cycle

These descriptions suggest that all projects have to pass through certain stages. Thus:

1. Projects have to be identified. For this, investment opportunity studies have to be made. Someone has to analyze the existing situation in the concerned local area, its resources, and constraints, and on the basis of the analysis, prepare a shelf or a pool of projects. This shelf or pool has to be screened to bring the choice of projects to manageable limits. Prefeasibility analyses have to be done in order to determine whether or not it is worthwhile to further examine the projects.
2. Projects need to be well prepared. In other words, their feasibility has to be carefully examined. Choices of scale, e.g., how much--irrigation extension to 500 ha or 1,000 ha--or how long--a 20 km road or 10 km road; choices of technology, e.g., two harvesters with five workers, or one harvester with twenty workers; and choices of location, e.g., village A or village B, have to be made. Firm estimates of costs and benefits of the preferred projects have to be made. Objectives of the projects have to be clearly defined. Institutional and social aspects of the project have also to be closely examined.
3. They require an appraisal. This stage is particularly relevant for projects seeking external funds. The funding agency has to satisfy itself that the net worth of the projects would justify the investments. It matters little whether the funding agency is a bank, a financing institution within the country, or a foreign bank such as the Asian Development Bank; every one of them would like to make their own appraisals before they agree to commit funding for them.
4. Projects would need to be designed for implementation. Someone has to prepare the drawings, the blueprints and the sequence in which the various activities concerning the projects will need to be carried out. Each single activity connected with the projects, particularly the most critical ones, has to be identified and programmed.
5. Projects have to be organized for implementation. Who will do what, through what kinds of control mechanism, and by what procedures and lines of authority, etc.? Clear delineation has to be established regarding these questions.
6. Projects need monitoring and progress reporting devices. Decisions on what aspects will be moni-

tored have to be made. What information will be required for this purpose? Who will be entrusted with this task? At what intervals would the progress on projects be reported?

7. Projects require evaluation mechanisms. How will projects be evaluated with respect to the objectives? What indicators will be used for this purpose? Who will be responsible for this activity?

These stages are shown in Figure 5.

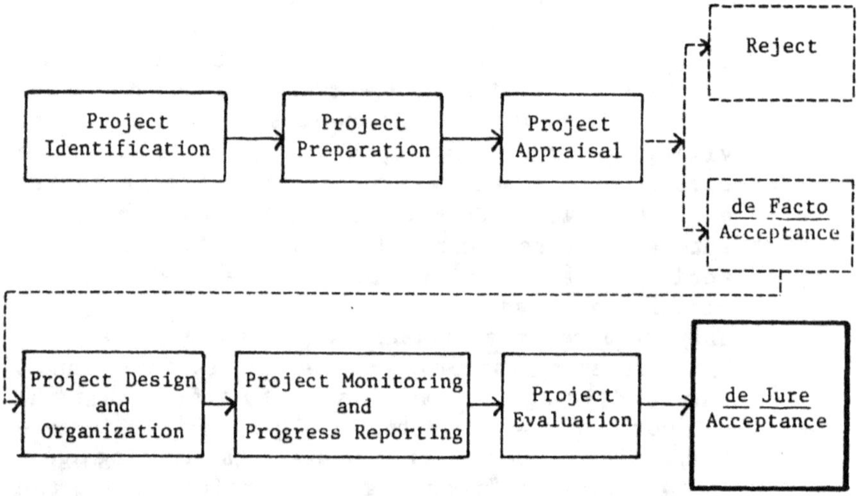

Figure 5. The project planning sequence (PPS)

The local level functionaries will not find this sequence any different from the one that is used for planning of relatively large-scale development projects. There is, in fact, no difference as far as the sequence or the stages are concerned. All projects--large or small, regional or local--have to traverse the entire sequence, although the degree of details as well as the rigor with which the various stages in the sequence may be dealt with may vary. It will be noted from the sequence in Figure 5 that projects can be accepted, at least in a de facto sense, once they have passed the appraisal and feasibility tests. A final decision on them, however, is desirable, even necessary, after they have been designed for implementation, and their organizational, monitoring, and evaluation details have been worked out. Experience shows that consideration of such details in advance of the *de jure* acceptance of the projects helps planners in making better decisions.

This book deals with only the first three stages of the project planning sequence. In regard to these stages, the book attempts to set out in detail the types of data that are necessary, how that data should be analyzed, and what conclusions should be drawn in order to reach decisions on the project's feasibility.

NOTES

1. See pages 10-12 for a discussion on the stages of project planning.

2. The World Bank, *World Development Report, 1982* (New York: Oxford University Press, 1982), p. 78.

> The 1980 Report [World Development] suggested that absolute poverty affected a total of about 780 million people, excluding China and other low-income centrally planned economies such as Vietnam. China's nationwide food security, along with basic health and education services, may blunt the impact of poverty; nevertheless, it is probable that at least 150 million people there enjoy living standards little better than those of the absolutely poor in other countries.

3. Government of the People's Republic of Bangladesh, Planning Commission, *The Second Five Year Plan 1980-85.* Dacca, May 1980.

4. J. Price Gittinger, *Economic Analysis of Agricultural Projects*, EDI Series in Economic Development, published for the Economic Development Institute of the World Bank (Baltimore and London: The Johns Hopkins Press, 1982), pp. 3-4.

5. A.A.M. Abdul Hye, "Local Level Planning in Bangladesh: Review of Past Experiences and Suggestions for the Future," (mimeo) December 1980, p. 91 (emphasis added by the author).

6. Dennis A. Rondinelli, "Project Identification in Economic Development," *Journal of World Trade Law*, Vol. 10, No. 3, May/June 1976.

7. Morris I. Solomon, *Analysis of Projects for Economic Growth* (New York: Praeger Special Studies, 1970), p. 15.

8. Gittinger, p. 5.

9. Hiran D. Dias and B.W.E. Wickramanayake, *Manual for*

Training in Rural Development Planning (Bangkok: Asian Institute of Technology, 1981) (mimeo), pp. F-4-5-6.

10. It should be understood that project planning is not a broad-spectrum remedy for all kinds of planning or development ills. It is one of the tools which, if properly used, can contribute to improving the decision-making process in the developing countries.

11. See, for instance, the Operational Guidelines for Preparation of IRD Block Plans, produced by the Ministry of Rural Reconstruction, Government of India (1980). These guidelines refer to steps necessary for the preparation of block plans but not of projects. The Thana Plan Book for Works Programme, on the other hand, provides guidelines for the preparation of projects but not for the formulation of Thana Plans.

12. I.M.D. Little and J. A. Mirrlees, Project Appraisal and Planning for Developing Countries (London: Heinemann Educational Books, 1974), pp. 81-87. Many other authors have begun to treat project preparation as a part of the overall planning process. See Ed. B. Prantilla and Md. Fazlul Haq, "The Process of Planning for Local Level Development," United Nations Centre for Regional Development, 1981 (Draft, pp. 18-22). The National Institute for Rural Development, Hyderabad, India, has included "Project Formulation" as one of the ten steps necessary for the preparation of block plans. See United Nations Economic and Social Commission for Asia and the Pacific, Guidelines for Local-Level Planning in Rural Areas, Report of National Workshops held in six Asian Countries, 1981.

13. United Nations Economic and Social Commission for Asia and the Pacific, Guidelines for Rural Centre Planning, New York, 1979.

14. Dennis A. Rondinelli and Aspy Palia, Project Planning and Implementation in Developing Countries: A Bibliography on Development Project Management (Honolulu: East-West Centre, 1976).

EXERCISES

1. Why do you think the developing countries pay so little attention to systematic project planning at local levels? Support your reply with specific instances that you may be aware of.

2. Trace the functional linkages of any project with which you are most familiar.

2
Identification of Projects

ENVIRONMENT FOR PROJECT IDENTIFICATION

Identification of projects that will contribute to the development of a given local area is one of the most critical tasks in project planning exercises. Almost everything depends upon the selection of the right kinds of projects. Thus, a proper search for them has to be made at the very beginning of any planning effort. But the task of searching for the right kinds of projects or generation of new projects, as it is often called in the vocabulary of planners, is not at all easy. Experience has shown that planners at the local level find it exceedingly difficult to come up with new project ideas. What they frequently propose is somewhat "repetitive" with the result that the problems plaguing local areas never get solved. Generally, it is "more of the same" types of projects that are selected. There is also a tendency among planners to view project identification as a linear function of the resources available in the area. We often find local level officers arguing that because their area is endowed with good livestock, a tannery should be started there. It is no surprise that a number of projects based on this kind of justification never take off the ground. Many projects stagnate; others die prematurely. Why does this happen? Why is the process of project identification so difficult?

There are several reasons for this, and even though many of the reasons might appear obvious, it is nevertheless necessary to explicitly recognize them. The first, and perhaps the most important reason is that a local area such as a Tambon, a Kabupaten, or a Block is part of a larger national system, and has to adopt and pursue certain guidelines, norms, and priorities laid down by the larger system, that is, the central government of the country. A local area is not entirely free in choosing its development path or priorities. It is bound by "externalities." The degree of freedom within which it can choose projects is constrained. The local area, in short, is not autonomous in its development actions. For instance, if a local area wishes to pursue a particular line of action which is of low priority to the central government of the country, there is almost no way in which it can do so without coming into conflict with the central government. Thus, some projects that, to a local area, may appear promising may not be able to be put up because of the guidelines/priority laid down from above. Conversely, if there is a program that enjoys a high order of priority at the central level there would hardly be any way in which a constituent local area could consciously disregard this priority.

Secondly, there is considerable fuzziness about development objectives in developing countries. Development plans include several kinds of goals and objectives, many being incompatible with each other. Often, there are tradeoffs between some of them. Apart from the fuzziness, seldom do the plans indicate many order of priorities among the various objectives. In the absence of inter se priority, proper identification of projects becomes an exceedingly difficult task for planners. Consider the dilemma of local level officers when they have to identify projects that would serve the following objectives--all at the same time (Fig. 6).

How to identify projects under this kind of a situation remains one of the major problems for local level planners.

Thirdly, the nature of planning in the developing countries affects the environment within which projects have to be identified. Planning in most developing countries is a blend of market forces and governmental intervention. For some sectors, the government relies on its own assessment of the economy, and based on the assessment makes appropriate resource allocations. In other spheres, it prefers to utilize the initiative of the private entrepreneurs by offering them a package of incentives, tax subsidies, rebates, seed money, etc. Identification of projects in a mixed system that operates on different planning principles requires a set of procedures that are not always easy to comprehend and operationalize.

Fourthly, a local area operates on limited information. Although this is a problem common to many developing countries, it is particularly acute in large, multiracial and multilingual countries and many newly independent countries

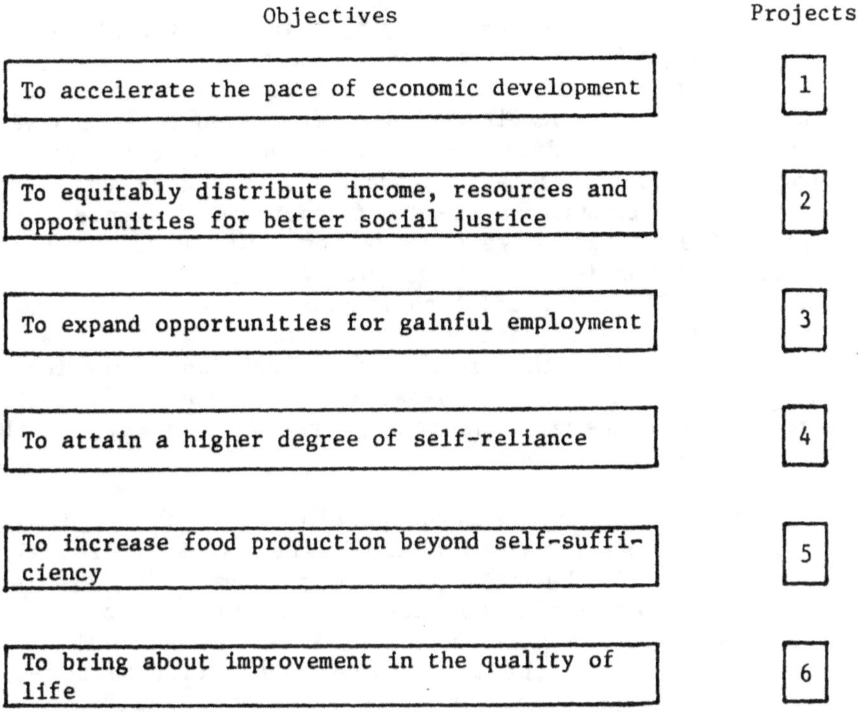

Figure 6. The planners' dilemma

in the Pacific, where information does not flow easily either among the constituent local units, or between units at various spatial levels. This lack of information grossly inhibits the capacity of local level functionaries for identification of projects. For example, it is unlikely that a particular Tambon or a Municipio will have reliable information on what the adjoining Tambons and Municipios are planning to do in the course of the next few years. For all one knows, they may also be thinking of a tannery project! Or, the area may have plans to set up a project for canning vegetables with the object of selling canned vegetables in the nearby markets. For this to materialize, however, this area will need to have market data from adjoining areas as well--information that it may or may not have. Lack of information and its limited flow, therefore, restrict the capacity of local level officers to identify really suitable projects for their specific localities.

Fifthly, the local level environment for project identification is constrained by pressures from various groups and sections of the community. It is a fact that the effects of a project vary from one group of people to another. An upstream irrigation project may bring benefits to farmers in the immediate locality but its effects on farmers living downstream may be disastrous. Some groups benefit from the project while others bear its cost. It has been noted that even within homogeneous areas the reactions of people to the value of a project have been varied. Clearly, the local level functionaries have to grapple with conflicts of interest, reconcile them, and then identify projects for careful consideration, which are not easy tasks.

And, finally, the process of project identification is made difficult by the very nature of the local areas that are, in most cases, inhabited by people who are, in the words of Robert Chambers,

> hard to reach and hard to help. They are typically unorganized, inarticulate, often sick, seasonally hungry, and dependent on local patrons. They are less educated, less in contact with communications, less likely to use government services, and less likely to visit outside their home area than their better-off rural neighbours. They are often especially concentrated in areas remote from urban centres. Further, they are relatively invisible. Urban-based officials and foreign experts alike can easily, as "rural development tourists", make rural visits without either seeing or speaking to the poorer people. Residentially, they are often separate. A week could be spent in South India visiting villages without even entering one of the harijan colonies where many of the very poorest live. In parts of Africa, roadside elites emerging as the richer people buy up the most desirable plots besides the roads and build good houses there, while the poorer people increasingly shift away out of sight. Visitors tend to see, to meet, and to interact with, only the more influential and better-off rural people.[1]

The identification of projects for this kind of a setting requires an altogether different approach than what we are normally accustomed to.

This is the general environment within which project identification takes place. An understanding of the environment helps the process of identification a great deal.

BASIC STEPS IN PROJECT IDENTIFICATION

Introduction to Investment Opportunity and Prefeasibility Study

It is generally true that before an idea matures or attains an identity of its own, it passes through several stages of examination and consideration. An idea is first born; it incubates for some time, and then it begins to take shape. In an almost identical manner, project ideas develop. This example can be seen in the context of any local area. Project ideas are generated by local level functionaries and other groups of people; these are screened in a preliminary fashion to weed out the obviously bad or impractical ones; and then a more systematic analysis is undertaken for projects that pass the screening test. This process consists of four steps that are shown in Figure 7.

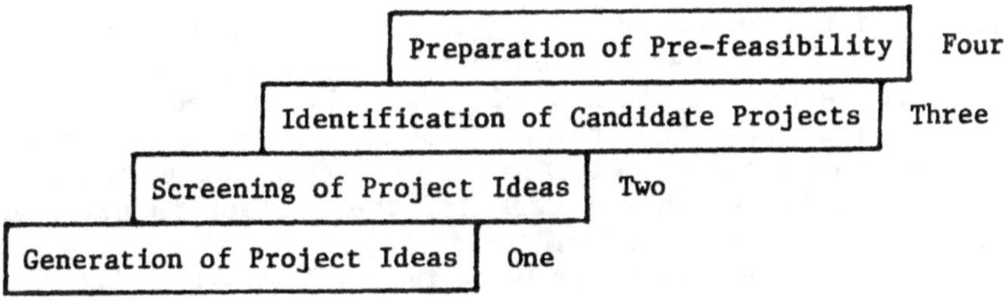

Figure 7. Steps in project identification

In textbooks, these steps have been discussed under the captions of the investment opportunity study (IOS) and prefeasibility study. The purpose of the investment opportunity study (one and two of Fig. 7) is to generate project ideas by examining the potentials, problems, and the needs and aspirations of the people in the concerned local area. What can possibly be done in the area? How can its development problems be solved? In what fashion can the economy of the area be transformed? How can the existing animal husbandry practices be changed? What should be done to involve women in the development process? In short, where do the development opportunities for the area lie? It is also the purpose of the investment opportunity study to examine, in general terms, the external and internal environment with a view to identify factors that are likely to either favor or impede development, with particular reference to the area concerned. The investment opportunity study is necessarily broad and somewhat sketchy, and meant in the first stage to provide planners with a choice of projects from which they may make a selection. Surely, not all projects evolved in this fashion would qualify. Some project ideas may be too fanciful for serious consideration. It is the stage when project ideas are screened and evaluated on the basis of certain criteria--that is, prior to their being put to additional tests of feasibility.

The prefeasibility study (three and four of Fig. 7) looks at the technical, financial, and other aspects of the "screened-in" projects, that is, those which emerge from the preceding step. These are often referred to as "candidate" projects. The purpose of the prefeasibility study is to determine, in general terms, whether or not there is enough justification for undertaking full-fledged feasibility studies of projects under consideration. Thus, if the examination of technical, financial, and other aspects of the project indicates that the project is likely to encounter problems of a technical, financial, or any other nature, then it is during this stage that the project is dropped from further consideration.

A prefeasibility study is an intermediate stage between an investment opportunity study and a detailed feasibility study--the difference being primarily about the details of the information required. According to the Manual for the Preparation of Industrial Feasibility Studies,[2] this stage is an important one in project planning as it helps in determining whether:

1. The investment opportunity is so promising that an investment decision can be taken on the basis of the information elaborated at the prefeasibility stage.
2. The project concept justifies a detailed analysis by a feasibility study.
3. Any aspects of the project are critical to its feasibility and necessitate in-depth investigation through studies such as market surveys.
4. The information is adequate to decide that the project idea is not either a viable proposition or attractive enough for potential investors.

These steps in project identification can be examined by addressing the following three questions:

1. Who generates projects? What is their source?
2. How are projects generated? What kinds of studies and surveys are necessary?
3. What exactly is involved in prefeasibility brief or study? How are data presented to enable local planners to arrive at decisions whether full-fledged feasibilities of the candiate projects should be prepared or not?

Sources of Projects

Who generates projects? This question appears obvious enough. Projects are generated by government agencies, credit institutions, nongovernmental organizations and the people (Fig. 8). The government, however, remains the single most important agency for generating projects. They have the necessary resources for this task. They have access to information that can lead to project ideas. They have the machinery for conducting surveys and need analyses to seek actively opportunities for investment and problem solving. And, finally, they are fully conversant with the development priorities and strategies. Of late, this particular source is being supplemented by the efforts of the credit and financing institutions and cooperatives. Their interest has been motivated by the increasing role they have been called upon to play in advancing credit to small and marginal farmers, and other disadvantaged groups. They have been conducting surveys and studies on their own to find out potential investment opportunities, thereby adding to the pool of project ideas. To these must be added the role of the people and nongovernmental organizations in identifying projects. This source is as yet not very active but there is an increasing realization that people have better and more intimate knowledge of their area's problems and opportunities, and that this knowledge should be made use of by the governmental machinery in identifying relevant projects. Different methods of involving the people in the project identification process have been employed in the developing countries, mention of which is made in several publications on the subject.[3]

The purpose of mobilizing the various sources is to obtain a cross section of ideas on projects. It is not adequate to have only the views of the government or the

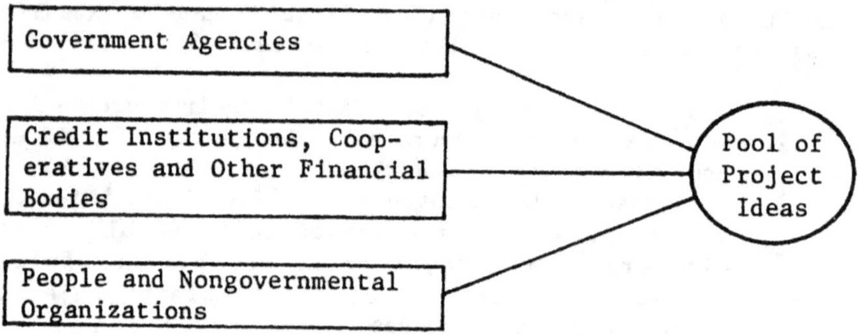

Figure 8. Sources of projects

people. All sources need to be tapped so that the pool is large as well as reflective of the people's needs, aspirations, and potentials. It is this pool that provides the first basis for local level functionaries to begin a systematic identification of projects.[4]

Studies and Surveys for Project Identification

How are projects identified? What kinds of surveys and studies are necessary?

At the outset, it should be mentioned that project generation and identification is a two-way process. One is what may be called a top-down process; the second is referred to as a bottom-up process. There is a third process, too--the participatory process that is assuming significance in many developing countries, although its precise contents and methodology are still in the process of evolution.

For an easy understanding of the top-down process of project identification, it is useful to refer to the situation of a local area, say a Upa-Zilla in Bangladesh, where, assume for a moment, the executive officer[5] has been entrusted with the task of formulating an Upa-Zilla Development Plan. The executive officer would take several steps. First, he would look into the national development plan, and examine the implications of certain specific national parameters (norms and values, development strategies and priorities, and constraints) for the development of his Upa-Zilla. Second, he would make a quick assessment of the development problems and potentials for his Upa-Zilla. It will be an extrinsic assessment to enable him to appreciate the key problems and potentialities. He might for this purpose conduct quick studies of important sectors. And third, he would ask for the views of the people and their representatives on the future development prospects and priorities of the Upa-Zilla. A synthesis of these steps would enable the executive officer to produce a loosely knit draft framework for the development of the Upa-Zilla, for a given period of time.[6] This framework would indicate the directions for development, priority areas, objectives, and the barriers to development. The framework may also give indications on the growth rates, sectoral targets, investment requirements, employment generation, and sometimes a broad content of the major programs. The mechanism of translating this framework into project ideas and investment action is what is called the top-down process of project identification. It is top-down because it emerges from the top, that is, the governmental machinery, and because almost the entire exercise involves acceptance of the draft plan framework as the basis for identification of projects. It is essentially a process of systematic thinking about projects that can contribute, in line with the directions spelled out in the framework, to the development of the local area. Figure 9 illustrates the top-down process of project identification.

As distinct from this approach where projects emerge from the draft plan framework, the bottom-up approach relies on extensive detailed surveys and analyses of the resources, needs and problems of the concerned area (Fig. 10). The main advantage of this approach is that it helps in locating exactly where in the concerned local area a specific need or problem exists. It provides information on the geographical distribution of the area's resources and potentialities. How much ground water, and where? Which part of the area is suited for which crops? Is the area endowed with specific skills? Which villages have the largest number of landless and unemployed? Which villages suffer most during monsoon floods? Does the area suffer from inadequate infrastructure? To what do the people of the area aspire? In short, the bottom-up approach provides disaggregated information on the area, and provides a spatial dimension to project identification.

The third approach, i.e., the participatory approach to project identification, is in its early stages of development. The basic idea underlying this approach is that at the local level it is far more meaningful and productive for various groups--the governmental machinery, representatives of the credit institutions, the nongovernmental organizations and the people to jointly determine the area's devel-

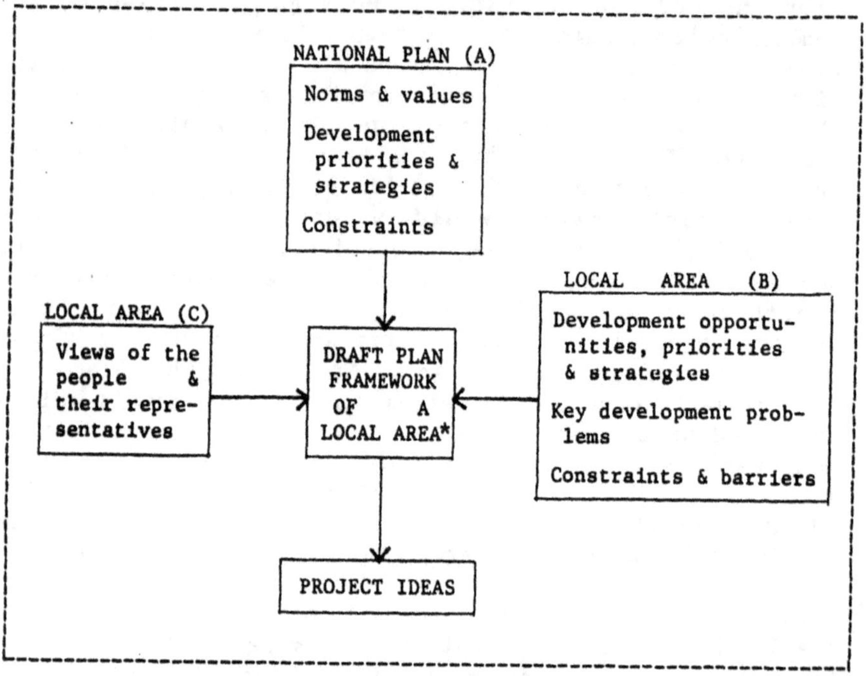

* Note: This is more often referred to as the macro development framework. Those who are interested in the methodology of constructing such a framework may refer to Bohdan Gruchman, "An International Review on the Methods of Macro-Framework Building for Comprehensive Regional Development" in Asian Development Dialogue, Nos. 5 and 6, 1978, United Nations Centre for Regional Development.

Figure 9. A top-down approach to project identification

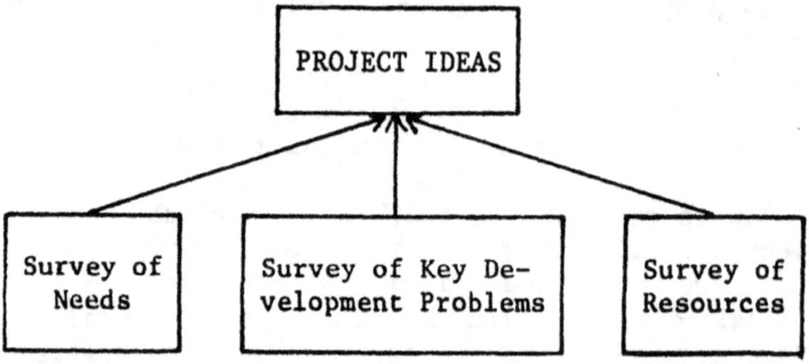

Figure 10. A bottom-up approach to project identification

opment objectives, strategy, and projects. That is, all those groups that have an interest in development should jointly participate in the exercise of project identification. The approach has been noted for many special features such as:

1. It is a low-cost device
2. It is time saving
3. It is likely to be more realistic in terms of identification of problems and projects
4. It helps in building consensus on key development issues
5. It facilitates implementation of programs and projects

A prerequisite for this kind of approach is the selection of the spatial unit. Too large a unit may not allow for a frank discussion on the area's most pressing needs. Likewise, too small a unit may not be able to generate enough ideas for its own development. Which of the three approaches would give better results is difficult to prejudge. Also, they are not mutually exclusive. Given the time and resources, an appropriate mix of the three can provide information on which a high degree of confidence can be placed. Where time and resources constitute a constraint --as is likely to be the case--a selection appropriate to the local situation will need to be made.

In any of the above approaches, or their combinations, some data will be required. Only data can provide the necessary base and reliability to local planners. Without data, there will always be an element of uncertainty and doubt in the minds of planners as to whether their assessment of the situation is right. Before indicating the types of data that are useful for this phase of a project planning exercise, two points concerning data collection should be taken note of. First, data collection is not a neutral exercise. It is closely related to the objectives one has in mind. In this sense, it is distinct from a statistical handbook. Thus, it is hardly useful for local level planners to collect all kinds of information. It is important to recognize this because in many developing countries either there is too much information or too little of it, or more often it is irrelevant to the aims in mind. On this subject, the comments of Robert Chambers are particularly relevant.

> In rural development, a great deal of the information that is generated is, in various combinations, irrelevant, late, wrong and/or unusable anyway. It also often costs a lot to obtain, process, analyse and digest. Although many professionals have given thought to improving information gathering it remains a remarkably inefficient activity. Criteria of cost-effectiveness do not appear often to have been applied, and manifest inefficiency is sometimes met by demanding not better information, or less, but simply more.[7]

This situation has to be avoided by making a careful selection of data that may be considered relevant.

The second point to be noted is that qualitative data are almost as reliable as quantitative. This is particularly so at local levels such as the Tambons, Barangys, or Kabupatens. Often, statistics are considered synonymous with accuracy, and plain statements and views with inaccuracy. Such a view needs to be completely discarded in local level planning where reliance has to be placed on people's views about what they perceive as local priorities or problems.

Several textbooks and professional papers have listed, in sufficient detail, the types of data that would be useful for project identification. In most cases, these are related to regional/national level projects.[8] For identification of local level projects two types of data would be necessary to be collected. The first type would consist of data that are external to the local area (Block A in Figure 9, p. 31), which would help planners in understanding the general development climate, including development priorities and strategies. The second type would comprise all data internal to the area concerned as shown in Blocks B and C of Figure 9. This should enable planners to fully comprehend the development problems as well as enable them to identify development possibilities and potentialities of the area concerned. Although data of the first type can be obtained by reviewing and examining the national/regional policies, plans, and programs, surveys at three levels will need to be conducted for generating data useful for project identification. These levels are:

1. Households
2. Villages/towns/settlements
3. Development institutions

The purpose of the household surveys is to obtain a clear understanding of the needs, aspirations and capabilities of the people. These surveys are designed to generate information on the standards of living of the people in the community: their income levels, employment structure, holdings and assets, access to services and facilities, and their social status. These surveys can provide useful information as to who does what in the community, and why have certain sections of the population been left out of the mainstream of development? Are there any social and cultural barriers affecting their development? Are the various services and facilities adequate? Do the people feel constrained because infrastructure is not adequately developed? What, in their opinion, are the priority areas? Household surveys are also reliable for assessing the value systems of the people and the kind of development style they would prefer to have.[9]

The object of village level surveys is to generate data on resources (land, water, fisheries, and animal stock), their present levels of utilization, the availability of and accessibility to economic services (markets, banks, storage facilities and nurseries), social facilities (health, education, family planning), and infrastructure (road, culverts, bridges, canals, irrigation channels, tube wells, etc.). They are resource surveys at the village level. Likewise, a survey of institutions such as the various types of organizations for specific groups (women, youth, weavers, fishermen, landless, jute growers, sugarcane growers, etc.) can give planners useful data on what their development priorities are, how each group perceives its problems, as well as how these problems can be effectively tackled.

Project ideas are generated through such surveys. The entire exercise requires considerable skill in conducting surveys, analyzing data, and compiling them for the use of planners. It is desirable to operate from several angles so as to obtain a wider perspective and projects that will reflect the needs, problems, and resources of the area. The total process of generating projects is summed up in Figure 11.

Clearly, not all projects generated in this fashion can be accepted. Rarely would there be enough financial resources to accommodate them. Also, many of them may not even be viable. In order to be considered for the next phase of the project's planning sequence, i.e., the preparation of the prefeasibility brief, all project ideas have to be processed and screened with respect to their priority to the local community. The purpose of "screening" is to

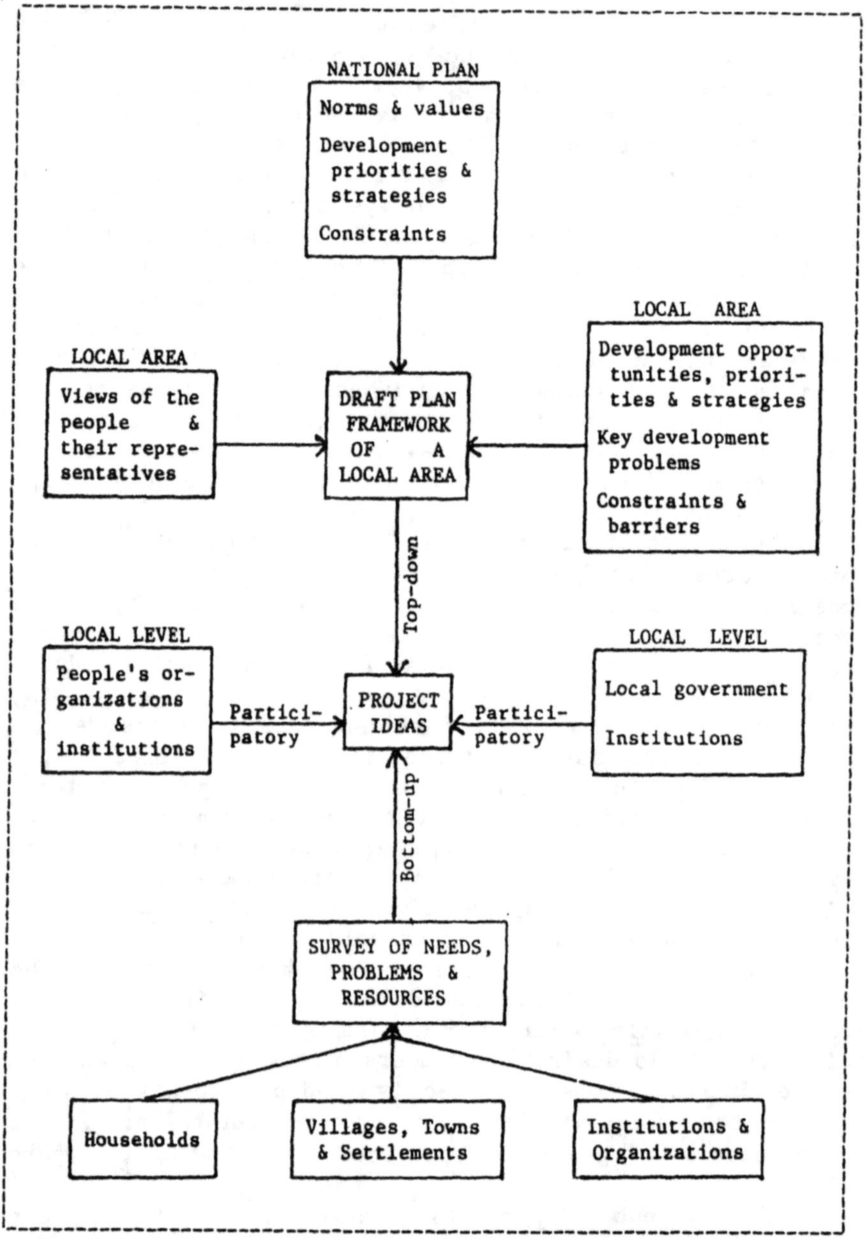

Figure 11. An integrated process of project identification

prioritize project ideas, to rank them in order that only those that rank high in terms of the needs and priorities of the local area are pursued further. For instance, it is quite conceivable that the pool may consist of projects that may result in the widening of disparities between the various sections of the community, or may benefit only a particular class, or may exacerbate large-scale migration from one to another part of the local area. There may be projects which, if accepted, may place demands on scarce resources, foreign exchange, etc. It is the purpose of the screening procedure to suggest how such and other projects should be viewed and ranked. Should these be pursued further or dropped from active consideration? The screening of projects is thus an important stage in resource allocation.

What is most important for this stage of project identification process is to develop a set of criteria for screening purposes, and to secure on this set the concurrence of the local community. The set of criteria has also to be consistent with the development priorities of the concerned local area. Thus, if poverty eradication is one of the main objectives of local development, then criteria such as the ones indicated below could be considered for screening the various project ideas:

1. __________ would/would not meet the absolute needs of the poorer sections of the local community.

2. __________ would/would not augment the earning capacity of the poorer sections of the local community.

3. __________ would/would not improve the accessibility of the poorer sections to basic communal services

4. __________ would/would not be located in the economically or socially depressed part of the local area.

Apart from screening of projects from the above viewpoint, it is useful to also extend the screening procedure for finding out which of them are likely to encounter problems in securing their requirements of various "inputs" such as raw materials, manpower, and finances, or in finding markets for their "outputs." Those expected to encounter problems of serious proportions can either be eliminated from further consideration or given low rankings. Questions of a general nature of which some examples are footnoted can provide appropriate responses to enable local level planners to take a view on their rankings.[10]

It is important to point out that the screening criteria are essentially soft and qualitative in nature, and are meant to eliminate low-priority projects, and admit those that merit further consideration of the planners. It is not a rigorous examination nor does it substitute the detailed examination of each and every candidate project that must remain an integral part of all project planning exercises.

Three sets of formats are provided on the following pages that might assist local level planners in screening project ideas. These are general enough to be adapted for specific use by local level planners in the countries.[11]

SELECTION OF TECHNOLOGY, SIZE, AND LOCATION FOR PROJECT IDENTIFICATION

While in general, the screening procedure described above establishes the stage for preparing prefeasibility briefs, there is one more important step to which serious attention should be given by local level planners. This step relates to making choices--choices with particular regard to:

1. The level of technology, i.e., the proportions in which machines (capital) and labor should be combined for the project in question.
2. The size or scale of the project, e.g., should the health clinic project be designed to serve a population of 5,000 or 1,000.
3. The location of the project, i.e., where should the project be located, in village A, or B, or in the headquarters of the local area.

The selection of the right combination of machines and labor, and the most appropriate size and location constitute an extremely important stage in project planning exercises. The reasons are not difficult to understand. For one thing, the costs of the projects and consequently their benefits vary with the level of technology, size, and their location. An example would amplify this point. Suppose the local agro-industries officer has under consideration a project for processing vegetables. He has already satisfied himself with respect to the availability of raw materials and the market, and has now to take a view whether or not he should initiate the preparation of a prefeasibility brief. In order to be able to take such a view, he would need information of various kinds: what techniques for processing vegetables are available and which ones he can possibly employ, that is, whether he should can the vegetables, or bottle

Format 1. Screening of Project Ideas According to the Priorities of the Concerned Local Area

Project Ideas Arranged According to Sectors/Sub-Sectors	Scales of Priority: High to Low		
	High	Medium	Low
Directly Productive Sectors			
Agriculture			
1			
2			
3			
Animal Husbandry/ Fisheries			
1			
2			
3			
Small-Scale Industries			
1			
2			
3			
Indirectly Productive Sectors			
Education			
1			
2			
3			
Health			
1			
2			
3			
Promotional Sectors			
1			
2			
3			

High:
Medium:
Low:

them or go in for dehydration; what capacity for the plant (quantities of vegetables) he should consider--50 kg, 100 kg, 200 kg; and of the locational choices available, which one appears to be the most advantageous.

Format 2. Screening of Project Ideas with Respect to Their "Inputs"

Project Ideas Arranged According to Sectors/Sub-Sectors	Do projects envisage any problems in securing inputs such as					
	Raw Materials		Manpower		Finances	
	No	Yes	No	Yes	No	Yes
<u>Directly Productive Sectors</u>						
Agriculture						
1						
2						
3						
Animal Husbandry/ Fisheries						
1						
2						
3						
Small-Scale Industries						
1						
2						
3						
<u>Indirectly Productive Sectors</u>						
Education						
1						
2						
3						
Health						
1						
2						
3						
<u>Promotional Sectors</u>						
1						
2						
3						

High:
Medium:
Low:

Without adequate information on these aspects, the decision-making capacity of the agro-industries officer would be severely limited. Dehydration of vegetables, for instance, would require a totally different process, a dif-

Format 3. Screening of Project Ideas with Respect to Their "Outputs"

Project Ideas Arranged According to Sectors/Sub-Sectors	Do the projects anticipate any problems in finding 'market' for their outputs-goods or services?	Do the projects require any promotional measures?
Directly Productive Sectors		
Agriculture		
1		
2		
3		
Animal Husbandry/ Fisheries		
1		
2		
3		
Small-Scale Industries		
1		
2		
3		
Indirectly Productive Sectors		
Education		
1		
2		
3		
Health		
1		
2		
3		
Promotional Sectors		
1		
2		
3		

High:
Medium:
Low:

ferent combination of machines and labor, and would certainly present an estimate of costs that would be different from the two other options, namely, the canning or bottling of vegetables. The alternative capacities of the plant would also have their own economics of costs; the cost per unit of processed vegetables may be high if the plant size is very small. On the other hand, market considerations may not permit the setting up of a plant of a larger capacity. Likewise, the location of the vegetable processing plant would influence the cost of the project.

The cost, however, is not the only reason the agro-industries officer has to consider these aspects. Quite often, the acceptability of the project by the authorities may depend on what technology has been proposed or what location has been suggested. If a project has been prepared on the basis of a technology that is either unavailable indigenously or available at prohibitive costs, the government may not be willing to accept it. Or, if the project proposal is prepared in such a way that it is likely to place heavier demands on scarce capital that is required for producing other priority goods and services, it may be given a low priority unless it is changed in such a way that it uses local labor in place of scarce capital. Similarly, a project may be rejected if its location is incompatible with the cultural traditions of the concerned local area. A tannery project would fall into this category.

These are, therefore, extremely important aspects in project analysis and planning. At the same time, none of these decisions are easy to arrive at, partly because choices or alternatives to choose from are far too many, and partly because the data, particularly the cost data for each of the alternatives, are not available. There are no formulae either that can provide planners the relative implications of each alternative. The process of optimization, that is, the method of identifying the "least-cost" option, is much too complicated to be used even for large, national-level projects, let alone for small-scale local-level projects. The local-level planners have, therefore, to understand and appreciate the general principles that underlie the selection of technology, size, and location, and apply them to projects under consideration with a view to obtaining the best possible judgment. It is important to note that the application of these principles will not provide clear answers as to what combination of machines and labor should be employed or what size should be selected; rather, it would provide cost and other implications of various choices that the local planners will need to consider within the overall development framework of the area/country. Reference to this aspect has already been made in the previous chapter.

Choice of Technology

As mentioned above, the choice of technology involves a decision on the proportion in which units of capital and labor should be combined. Whether to have five units of capital with twenty units of labor, or ten units of capital with five units of labor for a given project is the kind of decision that is involved in technology selection. It is evident here that what can be produced by five units of capital with twenty units of labor can also be produced by ten units of capital with five units of labor. Otherwise, it would not constitute a choice. Interestingly, such a choice is greater for local-level projects because capital and labor are more easily substitutable at that level. Even in projects where there is only one factor of production, say, labor, there would be a choice between various categories of labor such as five units of skilled labor with ten units of unskilled labor or ten units of skilled labor with two units of unskilled labor. Rarely will there be a project where such a choice does not exist.

In a broader sense, it would be obvious that the most important determinant of technology in any situation is the resource endowment--that is, the relative proportion in which labor, capital, land, skills, and natural resources are available to the area/economy. For an area that suffers from a relative shortage of capital and a relative abundance of labor (the typical situation of most developing countries), it would be preferable to choose a technology that uses more labor and less capital. This preference for labor-intensive technologies is based on the principle that greater use should be made of resources that are available in abundance in comparison with those whose availability and supply is limited. Because capital is a scarce resource in most developing countries, greater stress is placed on employing labor-intensive technologies so that labor can be fully and optimally utilized.

Having started this broad principle, it should be added that the question of technology decision making is by no means easy, and even though this has been one of the most widely written upon subjects, the range of agreement on how to arrive at the most appropriate technology remains rather limited. It is not at all easy to say how a technology decision should be made, what considerations should weigh in such decision making, what influences should be brought to bear, and what analytical framework should be applied. Louis Emmerij, in the Foreword to Amartya Sen's book,

Employment, Technology, and Development, has expressed the complex nature of the problem in the following words:

> The choice of technology is one of the key instruments of a development strategy, but the whole field of appropriate technology is still largely virgin for economists and engineers alike, since the hard facts about the possibilities of substituting labour for capital are hard to come by.[12]

The nonavailability of "hard facts" is not the only complicating feature of technology selection. Often there are pressures and compulsions of various kinds in the developing countries that compel them to adopt technologies that would normally be considered incompatible with their interests and resource endowment. In a recent paper, Benjamin Higgins has given the example of a city that opted for a capital-intensive water supply system over a labor-intensive design because first, labor skills to run the labor-intensive design were not available, and second, the authorities feared labor problems, which could not be afforded for such an important item of public utility.[13]

How, then, under these circumstances, should planners form their views on technology selection?

The International Labor Office has, in a study published under the title Technologies for Basic Needs, provided a set of criteria for technology selection. The study begins by pointing out that

> the actual criteria which should govern technology selection must differ from countries with different endowments, different objectives and different levels of development. Hence, desirable criteria can be listed only in a general way and with the reservation that governments may well attribute different weights to the various elements.[14]

It then suggests that technology should be selected in such a way as to:

1. have a high employment potential
2. have high productivity per unit of capital and other scarce resources
3. maximize the utilization of domestic materials, "especially of raw materials previously considered valueless"

4. be suitable for a scale of production warranted by the local markets, which are usually small and fragmented
5. have a low running cost, together with cheap and easy maintenance

The above set of criteria offers a reasonably simple guide for identification and selection of technologies for local level projects. It should be stressed that these criteria relate to the objective of maximizing productive employment; if the governments or local level planners have objectives other than this, then the criteria would obviously need to be different.

Size of the Project

Size of the project is the second factor that influences its costs and benefits. Should the size of a primary school project be 100 children or 200 children? Almost invariably, the local level functionaries are required to make such decisions: What should be the width of the road—4 m or 6 m; should the irrigation project cover an area of 100 ha, or 300 ha, or the entire village; and so on. How does one decide the appropriateness of the size? What kind of analysis is involved here?

There are at least two basic considerations that need to be looked at in determining the size of the project:

1. The type and nature of the demand expected to be met by the project. The first step in considering the size question is to find out the type of demand expected to be met by the project. Is the project being considered for meeting the gap in the "existing" demand, or the demand likely to arise in the next four or five years, or both? The example of a school project may once again be taken to elaborate the point. A primary school project is being considered as a candidate project by the local education officer. He will have several options to examine as far as the size of the project is concerned. First, he may prepare a project that would merely meet the gap in the existing demand for a primary school in the area. There are 100 children of primary school age (5-11 years) who are deprived of schooling because there is none in the area. The project may be designed to fulfill this need. Second, he may think of the future, say four or five years ahead, and prepare a

project in a way that it will have a capacity for admitting 100 children now, thirty children two years later, and another thirty-five children four years later. The first option takes account of only the existing demand whereas the second option takes note of the demand likely to arise in the near future. So, one of the factors in determining the size of the project is the time element: is the project aimed at meeting the existing demand, or the future demand, or both?

The question that planners face is how to estimate the future "demand" for the project or the service expected to be produced by the project. There are several methods available; however, only two are discussed here, as others are data intensive and involve fairly complex calculations.

a. Estimation of demand on the basis of past trends. This is one of the most useful techniques for estimating the future demand for any product or service. The technique implies that the future demand of the product or the service is determined by past growth trends. In other words, it means that the past growth trends will also persist into the future. By extrapolating the past trends, it is possible to estimate the future demand. Once the demand has been estimated, a view can be taken as to what share of the future demand should the candidate project plan to meet.

Two steps are involved in using this technique: (1) to find out the past growth rates; and (2) to extend the past growth rates into the future--more or less as a straight-line projection.

Take the case of a road project that envisages paving of a road that, at present, is a gravel road. One of the grounds on which paving of the gravel road can be justified is to show that the traffic on this road in the years to come will increase to such an extent that the gravel road will be unable to bear the increased traffic, and that paving would thus become necessary. The task of the planner in such a situation would be to realistically estimate the rate at which traffic on this road will increase in the future. For this to be estimated it is necessary to know the rate at which the traffic has increased in the past years.

Table 1 shows the increase in vehicular traffic between 1978 and 1983. There would be two ways of using these data for estimating the traffic in the years, say, 1984, 1985, 1986, and subsequent years. One way would be to find out from these data the simple (arithmetic) average rate of growth in traffic between 1978 and 1983. The second way

TABLE 1
Volume of traffic, 1978-1983

Year	Number of Vehicles
1978	100
1979	120
1980	150
1981	180
1982	225
1983	300

would be to calculate the compound (geometric) average rate of growth. The average growth rate is simple to calculate: between 1978 and 1983, the traffic grew to 300 vehicles from 100, or the absolute increase in the numbers of vehicles was 200 in a span of five years. In other words, on an average, 40 vehicles [(300-100)/5=40] were added to the traffic every year.[15]

For calculation of the compound (geometric) growth rate it would be necessary to use the compound interest rate formula. A calculator showing the y^x function may have to be used for calculating the compound growth raté, as shown below.

Given:
1. Vehicular traffic at the end of the period = 300
2. Vehicular traffic at the beginning of the period = 100
3. Total time or period (years) = 5

Equation:

$$300 = 100(1+r)^5$$
$$300/100 = (1+r)^5$$
$$3 = (1+r)^5$$
$$3^{1/5} = (1+r)$$
$$3y^x(1/5) = 1+r$$
$$1.246 = 1+r$$
$$1.246 - 1 = 0.246 = r$$
$$.246 \times 100 = 24.6\% \text{ annual growth rate}$$

By applying the two rates of growth, i.e., the simple and the compound averages, it is possible to estimate the vehicular traffic for 1984, 1985, and 1986. This may be seen from Table 2.

TABLE 2
Estimates of future traffic based on past trends

Year	Traffic Based on . . .	
	Simple average growth rate (40 vehicles/annually)	Compound growth rate (24.6% annually)
1984	340	374
1985	380	466
1986	420	580

This method of estimating future demand is very effective for projects involving roads, water supply, education, and similar service sectors.[16]

b. <u>Utilization of household budget studies for estimating future demand.</u> Utilization of household budget studies is another method that has been found to be effective in estimating demand for selected products and services at local levels. By means of this method it is possible to find out the changes in demand when either the income of the household or the price of the product undergoes a change. The method shows a quantitative relationship between the demand for the product and the household income, or the product's price, or both.

The expression of the relationship--referred to as (1) income elasticity and (2) price elasticity--is given in Note 17. It shows (a) the <u>rate</u> of change in demand when income rises or falls; and (b) the <u>rate</u> of change in demand when the price of the product goes up or down. By using the rate of change, it is possible to obtain an estimate of the future demand.

Tables 3 and 4 explain the use of the household budget data for estimating future demands. These tables show that:

1. There is a positive relationship between the household income and the demand for soap/household, i.e., when the income of the household increases, the demand for soap also increases.

TABLE 3
Change in the volume of demand when income changes

Year	Per Month Income/Household	Per Cent Change	Demand Per Month for Soap/Household	Per Cent Change
1980	Rs.500		5 kgs	
1981	Rs.550	10%	6 kgs	20%

TABLE 4
Change in the volume of demand when price changes

Year	Price/Unit	Per Cent Change	Demand Per Month for Soap/Household	Per Cent Change
1980	Rs.5/kg		5 kgs	
1981	Rs.6/kg	20%	3.5 kgs	30%

2. A 10 percent increase in household income results in a 20 percent rise in demand for soap.
3. A 20 percent increase in price of soap leads to a 30 percent decline in its demand. There is a negative correlation between the product's price and the demand for soap/household.

By using these relationships, it is possible to estimate the future demand for certain types of products. This method is more effective for those products that enter into the "consumption basket" of the household, and whose demands are linked up directly with the household incomes or the prices.

2. <u>The behavior of cost in relation to size of the project</u>. The second step in considering the question of size relates to the behavior of cost in relation to the size of the project. Does the unit cost of the project increase or decrease when the size of the project is changed? There would be several projects where the difference in unit cost

would be marginal with the change in the size of the project. In such a case, it would not pay to create capacity for future use. It would merely block the capital. On the other hand, if the project has substantial economies of scale, then a somewhat larger sized project with provisions to meet the future demand may be favorably acted upon if justified by the size of the market.

Although economies due to size are an extremely important consideration in determining the size of the project, these are far from easy to compute, and can hardly be expected to be estimated for local level projects. Perhaps, as a general guideline, it may suffice to bear in mind that the tendency to promote projects with larger capacities on the grounds of size economies often leads to a blocking of scarce capital, and should be curbed. The experience of many developing countries shows that a large number of projects suffer from blocked capital in the form of idle capacities. It is therefore necessary that the demand for the project is realistically assessed, and the size of the project determined on that basis.

Location of the Project

The third factor that influences the cost of the project is the location. The issue here is almost the same as in the case of technology or size. Location choices confront local planners for most projects, and it is not always clear which of the choices present a "least-cost" option. Take the case of a district where 10 km of primary roads are to be constructed in any given period of time. There would be several proposals: a road between Village A and Village B, or Village D and Village E, or Village D and District Headquarters, and so on. The costs and benefits of the three alternative proposals will hardly be the same. There would be topographical differences among these locations that would have a direct bearing on the cost of the road. A road between Village A and Village B may provide access to a relatively underdeveloped part of the district. Or, users of the three roads may be different. Each one of the factors would influence the costs and benefits of the three alternatives that have to be taken into account in project identification.

Take the example of a tannery project. For the tannery project, raw materials (hides, skins, tannin and other chemicals) have to be obtained. It involves the cost of transporting them to the proposed location of the project. Similarly, its outputs (finished skins and hides) have to be taken to the markets. Again, there is the transportation cost involved. The sum of the two costs, i.e., the cost of bringing the raw materials and the cost of transporting the finished products to the markets, will differ with locations, and consequently affect the calculation of the projects' costs and benefits. The task of the planners in the situation would be to obtain data on the total transportation costs for various alternative locations, and compare them in order to find out that location where the cost is lowest. Clearly, the location where the sum cost per unit of production is the lowest would be the most appropriate place for the project. However, not all projects fall into this category. There are many projects where the transportation cost as a proportion of total production cost is insignificant. It would mean that the project has no strong locational bias, and that the cost of the project will not be appreciably affected whichever location is chosen. These projects would be of "footloose" types. Also, there would be other categories of projects that have very strong location orientation. Quarrying is one such example. It is therefore important for local planners to understand (1) the nature of the project, and (2) whether transportation costs, e.g., raw materials and finished products, constitute a significant proportion of the total cost in order to determine the most appropriate location for the project under examination.

For the preparation of local development projects, all these factors, viz., the technology, the size, and the location, are extremely important, and have to be carefully reviewed as part of the project identification process. As explained above, there are several choices available. Methods to choose the most appropriate ones are soft, and much reliance has to be placed on the judgment of planners and administrators. It is important to recognize that the investments needed for one set of choices are different from another set, and likewise the outputs as related to the alternative choices are also different.

In order to be able to evaluate the implications of the various choices, it is best to develop simple formats such as given in Formats 4-6. These can be appropriately adapted for use in specific local situations.

Format 4. Selection of Technology for Candidate Projects

Choices of technology	Criteria for the Selection of Technology							
	Does it involve high-medium-low use of scarce resources?			Does it involve high-medium-low operational cost?			Is it difficult or easy to be replaced?	
	High	Medium	Low	High	Medium	low	Difficult	Easy
A								
B								
C								
D								

Format 5. Analysis of the Nature of Demand for Determining the Size of the Project

Nature of Demand for Determining the Size of the Project	Response	Description
Is the demand 'norm-oriented'? If yes, what are the norms?	yes/no	-----------
Is the demand related to population changes? If yes, what is the rate of population change expected, and what will be its effects on the demand?	yes/no	-----------
Is the demand sensitive to changes in incomes? If yes, what is the quantitative relationship between the rate of change in demand and variations in income?	yes/no	-----------
Is the demand sensitive to changes in prices? If yes, what is the quantitative relationship between the rate of change in demand and price variations?	yes/no	-----------

Format 6. Choosing Location for Candidate Projects

Choice of Locations	Factors that Affect the Choice of Location			
	Providing Access to the		Costs of Transporting Inputs & Outputs as a Proportion of the Total Production Costs	Economies of Concentration
	Disadvantaged Sections of the Community	Less Developed Parts of the Local Area		
A				
B				
C				
D				

PREFEASIBILITY BRIEF

What exactly is involved in preparing prefeasibility briefs of the projects? How are data presented to enable local planners to draw conclusions with respect to the feasibility of projects?

It was stated earlier in the chapter that prefeasibility is a systematic examination of those projects that emerge successfully from the screening process. It is a stage when projects are more concretely defined in terms of their general assessment of costs and benefits, purpose, main activities under them, the requirements of inputs, the potential contribution that projects can make to the area in general, and the sector/subsector in particular, and the main grounds for their justification. It constitutes a step forward toward decision making: to reject projects or prepare feasibility studies.

Preparation of a prefeasibility brief is an extremely important stage in project planning. Its significance can well be assessed from Colin Bruce's observations in his paper on "The Stages of Project Planning."

> Now project identification is not simply a matter of conceiving or thinking of ideas. Anybody with some knowledge and imagination can think of ideas for projects, and if the processes just outlined are followed a large number of project ideas are likely to be generated. But before time and resources are spent in following up these ideas in detail and carrying out feasibility studies, we need to have some feel for whether a project is likely to be feasible. So, we have to carry out some kind of prefeasibilty analysis in order to sift out the bad and the not-so-promising ideas, so as to concentrate one's scarce project preparation resources for more promising projects.
>
> The Brief (Prefeasibility) itself is, of course, a piece of paper and is the written culmination of the prefeasibility exercise. . . . The Project Identification Brief (PIB) . . . would define the objectives of the project, identify the constraints and the means for overcoming them, and make a rough and ready assessment of the costs and benefits. The purpose of preparing such a document is to seek approval in principle from management, serve as a basis for detailed preparation

> and provide the justification for committing scarce planning resources to detailed feasibility study and project preparation.[18]

In short, a prefeasibility brief is a digest of information for individual projects. It does not give all kinds of background data on the national policies or how projects fit into the overall national or regional priorities, but concentrates on such key information as would enable local planners and administrators to take a provisional decision on whether or not further work on projects is necessary. What is most important in preparing such briefs is that the key information for the project should be assembled and organized in such a manner that planners can see, almost at a glance, whether the project fits into their development framework or not. There are several ways in which this information can be organized; the following is one simple typology that might be useful for local development projects.

A. Introduction. A prefeasibilty brief should, at the outset, give the title of the project, the sector/subsector to which the project may belong, approximate data/month when work on the project may commence, and the expected period within which the project may become operational. It should also include an appropriate location for the project under consideration.

B. Purpose. This section should provide information on the long-range/short-range, and general/specific objectives of the project. It is important for planners to specify, and wherever possible, quantify the objectives of the project because the experience of many countries indicates that quite often, objectives are couched in such vague language that they mean very little; moreover, when the objectives are not specified clearly then the appraisal of the project becomes an exceedingly difficult task. There is also a tendency in many countries to overstate the objectives in order to get the project accepted. In this section, therefore, questions such as: What is the aim of the project? Whom will the project benefit? Who are the target groups or the expected beneficiaries? How many people will benefit from the project? Is the project aimed at solving the unemployment problem in the local area or improving the income distribution? This section should be dealt with as much precision as possible.

C. Activities and Specifications. Under this section, all activities under the project, small or big, should be clearly identified. Thus, for instance, a tube well irrigation project may entail digging the well, installation of motors, construction of channels, and so on. These will need to be identified, and clearly stated in the prefeasibility brief. Furthermore, specifications for each of them will also be required: the depth of the tube well, the horsepower of the motors, the width of the channels, the type of lining for the channels, etc.

D. Inputs and Requirements. This section should contain details on the estimated requirements of materials (cement, bricks, steel, machines, fuel, doors, tables, medicines, etc.), and manpower (labor, supervisors, engineers, doctors, teachers, extension workers) for the project. For most projects, the estimates will be of two types. The first type will be a one-time requirement. For instance, if there is a project that involves construction of a building, say a school, then cement, bricks, steel, etc. will constitute a one-time requirement. The second type will consist of recurring requirements which will include descriptions and quantities of materials that the project may require for its operation and maintenance.

This section should also indicate the organizational and institutional arrangements for the project. Who will execute the project? What kind of organizational arrangements will be necessary? Will the project require any major change in the existing setup? All such questions should be dealt with under this section.

E. Estimates of Costs and Benefits. The section should provide the best approximations of the total investment costs likely to be made in the project, as well as estimates of the total benefits, i.e., the value of the expected outputs. Like in the section on inputs, the investment costs of the project will need to be shown in two categories, namely: (1) the one-time costs, usually referred to as capital or fixed costs; and (2) recurring costs, that is, those that recur repeatedly. Recurring costs will be required to be shown on a year-to-year basis. This section should also give, wherever applicable, quantitative estimates of the benefits of the project on a yearly basis. Where it is not possible to impute money values, a description of the expected benefits should be provided.

F. Justification. This section should explain the principal justification for the project. There are many ways in which this can be done. For some types of projects it would be necessary to argue that the proposed projects would generate higher cash incomes for the poorer sections of the community, which are absolutely essential for their economic uplift. Some projects may need to be justified on the ground that they would bring about the necessary change in the attitude of the people without which the local area may continue to be mired in backwardness. For other types, particularly those whose outputs are measureable, justification may need to be given in terms of benefits and costs. Whatever may be the best form of providing justification, it is important that it is spelled out as clearly as possible so as to provide planners a basis for making the decision as to whether work on the project should be continued or not.

The preparation of prefeasibility briefs requires quite a different set of data. It requires, first of all, technical data. What types of machines and labor would be required for the various activities under the project? What specifications, e.g., horsepower of the motors; thickness of the walls; proportions in which cement, concrete, and sand should be mixed; etc., would be appropriate? How much energy (fuel, kerosene, and oil) would be needed for the various operations of the project? Such details are essential for most projects, in particular those that have a component involving construction. Take, for example, a project for the construction of a school. The planners concerned with this project will need to know how much steel, cement, bricks, and wood will be needed for the construction of the school. Without this information, the cost of the project cannot be assessed. Or, consider another project, which aims at involving the disadvantaged groups in raising their cash incomes through poultry raising or other similar activities. It will be essential to obtain data on various aspects of poultry raising. For instance, it will be necessary to know the quantity and quality of feed requirements for the poultry. At what intervals should the poultry be fed? What measures should be taken to keep the poultry infection free? And so on. This is a task that is done best by the concerned sectoral functionaries because the activities and the material requirements vary from project to project, and only they have the necessary competence to assess the varying technical requirements.

Secondly, manpower data are required for the preparation of prefeasibility briefs. These consist of the number and categories of manpower (professional, technical, skilled and unskilled) for the different operations of the project.

Thirdly, the preparation of prefeasibility briefs require cost data. Each activity under the project has to be costed as realistically as possible. There has been observed a widespread tendency in the developing countries to underestimate the costs in order to get the projects approved, with the result that projects experience interminable delays in their execution for want of adequate funds. This tendency has, therefore, to be checked. It is also important for planners to make separate estimates for capital costs requirements, and for maintenance and recurring costs, because here too, it has been noted that although capital costs are clearly identified and well taken care of by most projects, little attention is paid to estimating the maintenance and recurring costs. The result of improper costing, as we can see in many countries, is that buildings are constructed but there are insufficient funds to maintain and run the activities for which they were originally constructed. Separate estimates for each of the cost items are, therefore, essential as well as useful.

And finally, data on the output side of the projects have to be estimated. What will be the estimated value of the output of the project, if the output is measureable in money terms? If it is not measureable, then it will be necessary to provide a description of the output (number of students likely to attend the school, or number of patients expected to be treated at the health center, etc.). In making estimates of the output side, too, it will be necessary for planners to be realistic as there is usually a tendency to overstate the output in order to get the projects approved.

The above sets of data are a prerequisite for preparing prefeasibility briefs. It is through these sets of data that local planners are able to take the process of project selection one step closer to final decision. These data constitute the foundation for further analysis of the candidate projects.

Included in this chapter are two sets of formats that may be used by local planners in organizing the prefeasibility briefs. Format 7 may be used for individual projects, and Format 8 can be used for summarizing the same information for all projects under consideration.

One last observation needs to be made on situations when a systematic identification of projects involving studies, surveys, data collection, etc. may not be necessary. There are two such situations that are relevant at local levels. One is when the need for a project is obvious enough. An example may be given of a village or group of villages that have no access to, say, health centers or clinics within a radius of 30-40 km; or that they have no source of water supply that can provide water on a continuous basis. The need for a health clinic/water supply would then be obvious. By asking the villagers how intense their needs are, or by inquiring which of the two they would prefer to have if there were a choice, the cause of project planning is not strengthened in any appreciable manner.

The second situation is when a contingency situation arises, and merits immediate attention. Local functionaries often encounter contingencies of various types: flood, drought, breakdown in communication, failure of crops, sudden fall in the prices for agricultural produce, epidemics, etc. Projects have to be identified on an expediency basis to deal with such contingencies. Some data on the location of the affected area, magnitude of the problem, and the effectiveness of alternative solutions are, of course, necessary and should be obtained on a firefighting basis, but collection of more comprehensive data on the frequency of the occurrence of such problems, and the reactions of the people to alternative ways of solving the problems, cannot be afforded under the circumstances. It is a contingency situation, and needs to be tackled accordingly.

Not every local project needs extensive data or the preparation of prefeasibility briefs. At the same time, there is no substitute for a systematic examination of projects' feasibility before the government commits its scarce resources for the project.

In conclusion, it may be reiterated that project identification is the most critical stage in planning, and yet its methods are soft, and not fully tested against their results. Dennis Rondinelli notes that

> although project identificaiton is a seminal element of development administration, the literature is nearly void of systematic descriptions of how development projects are conceived, identified and defined. Scattered cases and project histories allude to sources of individual ventures, but little attempt has been made to provide an overview of project generation as a critical stage in planning and administration.[19]

Format 7. Prefeasibility Brief for a Candidate Project

A

INTRODUCTION

Title of the Project

Sector

Main

Subsidiary

Period

Preparatory time

Onstream date

Location

B

PURPOSE

Objectives

Long-range/General

Immediate/Specific

Targets

For Whom

Main users of the projects' output

Specific target groups or beneficiaries

C

ACTIVITIES AND SPECIFICATIONS

Principal Activities

Subsidiary Activities

Activity Specifications

Format 7. (Cont.)

D

INPUTS AND REQUIREMENTS[20/]

A. One-Time Requirements

(a) Construction materials

Steel

Cement

Bricks

(b) Machinery and equipment

B. Recurring Requirements

(a) Material requirements

Seeds

Fertilizers

Tar-coal

Medicines

(b) Infrastructure requirements

Fuel

Coal

Kerosene

Water supply

(c) Manpower requirements

Managerial

Professional

Technical/Skilled

Semi-skilled/Unskilled

Format 7. (Cont.)

E

ESTIMATES OF COSTS AND BENEFITS

<u>One-Time Capital Costs</u>

Construction materials

Machinery and equipment

<u>Recurring Costs</u> (on a year to year basis)

Material requirements

Infrastructure requirements

Manpower requirements

<u>Other Recurring Costs</u>

Taxes

Levies

Interest

<u>Benefits</u> (on a year to year basis)

Value of outputs

Description of outputs where these cannot be measured in money terms

<u>Other Benefits</u>

Subsidies

Rebates

F

JUSTIFICATION

Format 8. Summary of Prefeasibility Briefs for Candidate Projects

A. INTRODUCTION

Title of the Project	Sector/Subsector	Preparatory Time	Onstream Date	Proposed Location
1				
2				
3				
4				
5				

Format 8. (Cont.)

B. PURPOSE

Objectives		Targets	For Whom	
Long Range/General	Immediate/Specific		Main Users	Specific Target Groups
1				
2				
3				
4				
5				

Format 8. (Cont.)

C. ACTIVITIES AND SPECIFICATIONS

Principal Activities	Subsidiary Activities	Specifications
1		
2		
3		
4		
5		

Format 8. (Cont.)

D. INPUTS AND REQUIREMENTS - ONE-TIME REQUIREMENTS[20]

Construction Materials					Machinery and Equipment				
(1)	(2)	(3)	(4)	(5)	(1)	(2)	(3)	(4)	(5)
1									
2									
3									
4									
5									

Format 8. (Cont.)

D. INPUTS AND REQUIREMENTS - RECURRING REQUIREMENTS

Material Requirements				Infrastructure Requirements				Manpower Requirements			
(1)	(2)	(3)	(4)	(1)	(2)	(3)	(4)	(1)	(2)	(3)	(4)
1											
2											
3											
4											
5											

Format 8. (Cont.)

E. ESTIMATES OF COSTS AND BENEFITS

One-Time Capital Costs			Recurring Costs			Other Recurring Costs			Benefits		Other Benefits		
(1)	(2)	(3)	(1)	(2)	(3)	(1)	(2)	(3)	(1)	(2)	(1)	(2)	(3)
1													
2													
3													
4													
5													

Format 8. (Cont.)

F. JUSTIFICATION

1
2
3
4
5

NOTES

1. Robert Chambers, "Simple is Practical: Approaches and Realities for Project Selection for Poverty-Focused Rural Development," paper presented to the Seminar on the Implications of the Employment and Income Distribution Objectives for Project Appraisal and Identification, Kuwait, 5-6 April 1977.

2. United Nations Industrial Development Organization, Manual for the Preparation of Industrial Feasibility Studies, New York, 1978.

3. Of the various approaches for involving people, the following are of particular significance: (1) one-on-one approach, (2) communication with community leaders, (3) interaction through community meetings, (4) interaction with representative community and multivillage organizations, and (5) interaction with representative functional organizations.

4. Dennis Rondinelli writes that projects are generated through complex interactions among a variety of forces. A project identified by one means may, in fact, emerge from more than one source. The sources may also vary along at least four dimensional characteristics: (1) point of organization such as government agency, private organization or international body; (2) degree of formality; (3) degree of initiative; and (4) degree of centralized control. See his "Project Identification in Economic Development," Journal of World Trade Law, Vol. 10, No. 3, May/June 1976.

5. The Upa-Zilla Executive Officer is responsible for coordinating all development activities at the Upa-Zilla level in Bangladesh.

6. More often, this framework will consist of a few loose sheets; in a very few cases would there be a written, bound and published document.

7. Robert Chambers, "Rapid Rural Appraisal: Rationale and Repertoire presented to the World Bank Agricultural Sector Symposia, January 1980 (mimeo).

8. A recent publication of the United Nations has suggested that investment opportunity studies should consist of (1) an area study, (2) a subsector study, and (3) a resource-based oportunity study. Data requirements for an area study include: basic features of the area; population, occupational pattern, and socioeconomic background of the area set in the context of the country's socioeconomic structure; basic exploited and potentially exploitable production factors; a checklist of industries that can be developed on the basis of the available resources and infra-

structure facilities, etc. For subsector study, the publication suggests that data on the place and role of subsector as well as the size, structure, and growth rate for the subsector would be useful for purposes of project identification. See United Nations, Manual for the Preparation of Industrial Feasibility Studies, New York, 1978. Also see Colin Bruce, "The Stages of Project Planning: An Introduction to Project Planning," Economic Development Institute Training Materials, (Washington, D.C.: The International Bank for Reconstruction and Development), 1980.

9. According to Colin Bruce, ibid., p. 16,

> How do we find out what people want? This is not an easy question to answer because the answers must be very country-specific. Here are some possible ones. First, clearly some project ideas do come already and will continue to come to planning units via the politicians. The problem with this route, though, is often that the ideas get translated into decisions and handed down as instructions to proceed with such and such a project, without adequate identification and preparation processes being followed. Second, one can devise and carry out attitudinal sample surveys of wants, perhaps in conjunction with surveys of the socio-economic conditions of villages or rural areas, so as to be able to measure the demands against what is already being supplied or what is available. Such sample surveys can be very valuable, but they are expensive, and care needs to be exercised in getting the right sampling frame, devising the attitudinal questions and in interpreting the answers. Third, if project ideas at the grass roots level are to be properly investigated, prepared and appraised, then it is certainly highly desirable that there be project planning units within the public sector structure as close as possible to the grass roots level. How close to the grass roots level, how many of them there can be and what their relationships will be to higher planning levels are very country-specific questions which can be answered only in terms of specific constitutions, administrative levels, civil service organizations, size of countries and financial resources.

10. Are raw materials needed for the projects easily available? Will manpower of the types needed be available in the area? Will adequate finances be available for taking up and maintaining projects? Will projects place undue demands on scarce resources? Will there be an adequate demand for the "outputs" of the project? Can these be

easily marketed? Will there be enough traffic to justify road projects? Can the storage facility be used throughout the year?

11. The Training Module on "Formulating Local Level Development Projects," Module 4 (ed. B. Prantilla), presented at the Workshop on Local Level Planning Through Community Participation, held at the Pakistan Academy of Rural Development, Peshawar (1-19 March 1983), set out the projects screening criteria in a tabular form which is reproduced here:

Prototype Screening Criteria for Project Ideas at the Local Level, by Sector

Project title	Degree by which the project contributes to sector objectives	Degree by which the project contributes towards the solution of problem of the target group	Degree of resource use	Total score
(1)	(2)	(3)	(4)	(5)
1				
2				
3				
4				
5				

12. Amartya Sen, <u>Employment, Technology, and Development</u> (Oxford: Clarendon Press, 1975), p. v.

13. Benjamin Higgins, "Appropriate Technology: Does it Exist?" in <u>Regional Development Dialogue</u> (Nagoya, Japan: United Nations Centre for Regional Development), Vol. 3, No. 1, Spring 1982.

14. Hans Singer, <u>Technologies for Basic Needs</u> (Geneva: International Labour Office, 1977), p. 32.

15. For computing the rate of change, the following formula may be used:

Rate of change =

$$\frac{\left(\text{Value at the end of the period}\right) - \left(\text{Value at the beginning of the period}\right)}{\left(\text{Value at the beginning of the period}\right)} \Big/ \left(\text{Total period or number of years}\right)$$

16. In many countries, the demand for projects in the infrastructure and services sectors is determined on the basis of certain "norms" that are periodically laid down by the respective governments, e.g., all villages that have a population of 1,500 or more should be connected by a primary road, or for every 10,000 population, there should be a health subcenter, etc., are the types of norms that often constitute parts of the development plans and programs.

17.

Income Elasticity $$E = \frac{\frac{\Delta Q}{Q}}{\frac{\Delta R}{R}} \quad \text{i.e.,} \quad \frac{\text{Relative change in the volume of deman}}{\text{Relative change in income}}$$

Price Elasticity $$e = \frac{\frac{\Delta Q}{Q}}{\frac{\Delta P}{P}} \quad \text{i.e.,} \quad \frac{\text{Relative change in the volume of demand}}{\text{Relative change in price}}$$

18. See Colin Bruce, "The Stages of Project Planning."

19. Dennis A. Rondinelli, "Project Identification in Economic Development."

20. In recording inputs and requirements, distinction should be made between resources that are (a) locally available, (b) indigenously (within the country) available, and (c) externally available.

EXERCISES

1. What criteria would you recommend for screening minor irrigation projects? Note that the criteria given in Formats 1-3 are broad, and meant to indicate the process of screening rather than actual sets for use in any specific local area.

   You may use the same format for listing out the screening criteria.

Screening Criteria	Projects				
	1	2	3	4	5
Priority					
Inputs					
Outputs					
Any Other Criterion					

2. The following table provides time-series population data of a specific block in India. It is estimated that 23 percent of the population is school-going. Calculate the rates, both simple and compound, at which school-going population has increased during the past five years. Also estimate the school-going population for the next three years.

Year	Total Population	School-Going Population 23% of the Total	Rate of Growth	
			Simple	Compound
1	40,363			
2	42,801			
3	44,360			
4	46,700			
5	49,005			
6				
7				
8				

3. Identify the main items of costs and benefits for a health center project.

Costs	Benefits

4. Draft a prefeasibility brief for a road project for submission to the District Transport Officer. You may use data given in Exercise Case on Paving the Gravel Road given in Chapter 3.

3
Profitability in Project Analysis

WHY IS PROFITABILITY IMPORTANT?

Whatever may be the type of project--an irrigation project or the construction of a primary road, or the setting up of a health center, the aspect that concerns local planners and administrators most is whether the investment to be made in the project will pay off or not. Almost the entire attention of planners eventually becomes focused on this issue: Will the project be profitable? Will the investment in the project be effective? Will it be a worthwhile investment? It is obvious that if a project is unlikely to be profitable in the sense of its outputs (what the project produces) exceeding inputs (what the project consumes), it would be imprudent to invest in it. The argument is simple: a project must add to the "resources" of the economy--if it is unlikely to do so, then it should be discarded.

While the above argument is widely accepted, a number of problems are faced by planners and administrators in coming to grips with the concept of profitability. In fact, no other aspect of project planning has generated so much heat and discussion as this one, and despite considerable work done by several international organizations and individual experts, there exists today widespread disagreement and confusion on exactly what profitability is, and how it should be measured.

By and large, discussion on this aspect has centered around three questions:

1. What is the notion of profitability? Can we say that what is profitable to a private entrepreneur is also profitable to the government? In other

words, is there any basic difference in the manner a private entrepreneur looks at profitability and the way in which the government or society as a whole looks at it?

2. What methods can be employed to measure profitability? What kind of analysis is involved in this exercise? What if the project yields different levels of profits in different years? How should one determine the profitability of such a project?
3. How should the profitability of projects that do not yield profits in a monetary or financial sense, such as schools, health centers, low-income housing, and other social sector projects be measured?

Each one of these questions is of central importance to project analysis and planning; indeed, it is hardly ever possible to take a final decision on a project without looking at its "profitability." It remains the most crucial test in project selection.

NOTION OF PROFITABILITY

What is the notion of profitability? Can we say that what is profitable to a private entrepreneur is also profitable to the government?

In a general sense, a project is considered to be earning a profit--a kind of surplus--if the money value of its outputs, that is, what the project produces, is greater than the value of its inputs, that is, what the project consumes by way of raw materials, fuel, labor costs, etc., as shown in Figure 12. If the value of outputs is less than the value of inputs, then the project is not adding to the resources of the investor. In fact, the resources of the investor may be getting depleted. In such a case, the project is creating no surplus, and should prima facie be rejected.

Within this broad framework, the perspective of a private entrepreneur emerges somewhat more clearly. His interest lies in the difference between the value of the project's output, that is, the total receipts through sales, and the value of the project's inputs, i.e., the total payments. He would like to invest in a project that maximizes the difference between the receipts and payments, or the difference as a proportion of the investments. He would be less concerned as to whether the project increases the pressure on the country's scarce resources or diverts them from

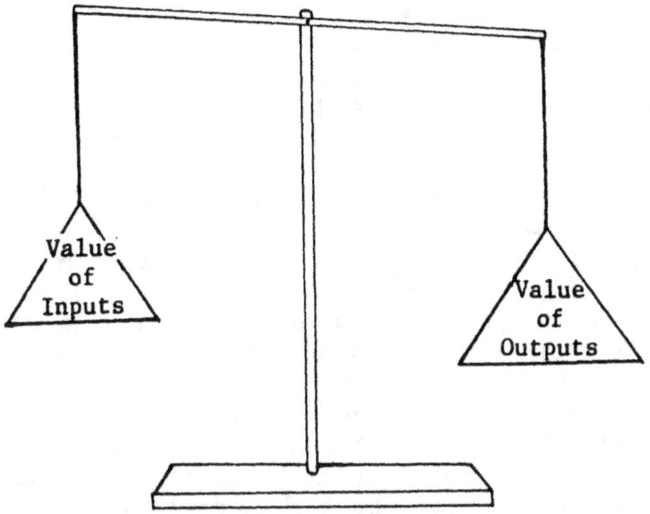

Figure 12. Weighing values of inputs and outputs

priority to nonpriority uses; or whether the project meets the requirements of a few rich or the poor masses; or whether on account of the project some sections of the community are adversely affected. He would aim at maximizing his personal gains by enhancing the rate of return on his investments. His interests are largely self-centered, although there would certainly be exceptions to this general rule.

The government operates on a different plane and pursues different interests altogether. The main aim of the government is to choose projects that will help in the attainment of various development objectives such as the increase in national income; expansion of employment opportunities; equitable distribution of incomes; provision of basic needs; meeting the needs of the disadvantaged sections of the community, etc. For the government, projects are instruments through which it operates to achieve its goals and objectives. Any project that does not contribute to such objectives is not "profitable" from the viewpoint of the government and, if selected, will entail a wasteful use of resources. The government represents the preference of the society, and therefore is interested not only in the direct effects of the projects but their total effects on the economy. It aims not at the maximization of the difference between the project's monetary earnings and payments (although this could well be one of the principal objectives), but at the total net gains of the projects. If, on account of the project, certain sections of the community are likely to be adversely affected, then it is an item of "cost" in the economic appraisal of the concerned project. On the other hand, if the project is likely to reduce income disparities in a given area, it is a "benefit" attributable to the project.

What difference the above explanation makes to the calculation of a project's profitability is obviously the most important question that confronts local level planners and administrators. The question can be posed more concretely in the following manner: if a planner has to appraise a minor irrigation project and calculate its profitability from his department's viewpoint, what items of costs and benefits would be taken into account? Would these items be any different from those that would show up, for instance, in the calculation sheet of a private entrepreneur? Whether the techniques of appraisal be the same or different?

It should be pointed out that the two ways of looking at profitability have been explained in project planning literature, in terms of (1) financial analysis and (2) economic analysis. Financial analysis deals with the monetary difference between the project's earnings and payments. It forms the core of profitability analysis, and is the main anchor to appraising projects from the viewpoint of the private entrepreneurs. Economic analysis looks at the project from the point of view of its expected contribution to the economy as a whole. Recent literature has argued that it is necessary to carry out both types of analyses for all projects under consideration, and it should not matter whether the project falls within the jurisdiction of private entrepreneurs or the government departments; the resources belong to the society as a whole, and should be used for the subservience of the interests of the society.

Let us return to the question: Where exactly do the differences between financial and economic analysis lie, and how crucial are the differences for planning of local development projects? Although there are several points of difference between financial and economic analysis, at least three of them are important enough to be noted and understood by local level planners and administrators. The first difference is that the items of costs and benefits are not the same under the two types of analyses. Under financial analysis, costs include all payments that reduce the money resources of the project, and benefits include all receipts that increase the project's monetary resources. For the economy, on the other hand, costs include only those payments that reduce the real resources while benefits include receipts that increase the real resources of the project. The difference between the money and real resources lies in the fact that there are certain payments and receipts that are in the nature of transfers from one section to another in the society, and do not in any way affect the total availability of resources to the economy as a whole. Taxes and various forms of subsidies and incentives are examples of such transfer payments and receipts, and would evidently fall outside of the scope of economic analysis. On the other hand, these payments and receipts are an integral part of financial analysis as they change the availability of financial or monetary resources of the projects under consideration. It should be pointed out that the primary interest of the private entrepreneurs lies in only the financial analysis; they are seldom concerned with the effects that their projects would have on the real resources of the society.

Financial Analysis:	Considers all monetary transactions
Economic Analysis:	Considers only those transactions that affect the resources of the economy Thus, it excludes all payments and receipts that constitute transfers from one section to other section of the community

A second difference--and a very important one between economic and financial analysis is concerned with the prices at which the inputs and outputs should be valued. There are the existing prices in the market. Cement is being sold at TK200/sack; steel at TK7,000/ton; wages of unskilled labor at TK10/day; foreign exchange at TK25/US$, and so on. Financial analysis of projects would obviously be based on these prices. These are the prices that the project will need to pay in order to acquire cement, steel, foreign exchange, etc. The question, however, arises as to whether these prices should be used in appraising projects from the point of view of the economy? Or should these prices be "corrected"? It is argued that the prices that prevail in the market are those that are fixed by the governments without taking full note of the demand for and supply of these commodities. These are the results of the various types of regulations and controls rather than the demand-supply interactions. If the market is left free of such controls, then the prices of factors such as foreign exchange, capital and labor would be quite different.

An example will make this clear. Consider labor wages. In many countries, a minimum wage ceiling is laid down below which labor cannot be hired even though it may be available. In financial analysis, the cost of the labor would be equal to the wages expected to be paid, which would, in most if not all cases, be the same as the minimum wage ceiling. For the economy, the real cost of the labor is less than the money cost because it can be acquired at wages lower than the ceiling. It is not a scarce factor of production but has been deliberately overpriced by the government. Likewise, the exchange rate between the local currency of a country and the foreign currency such as the US$ or the West German mark may be fixed in such a way that the value of the foreign currency is kept underpriced. The real value of foreign currency to the society, however, is much higher than that shown by the official exchange rate.

Because of the over- and underpricing that is a common phenomenon in most developing countries, it is suggested that in economic analyses of projects, planners should use not the market prices but the corrected, or the "shadow" or the "accounting" prices, as these are generaly called. Corrections to the market prices should be made in such a way that the corrected prices would reflect the relative scarcities of the main factors of production such as the foreign exchange, labor, capital, etc., as these alone can provide a correct assessment of the projects' contribution to the economy.[1]

Financial Analysis:	Values inputs and outputs at market prices
Economic Analysis:	Values inputs and outputs at shadow or accounting prices

Thirdly, the economic analysis is concerned with the sum effects of the concerned projects on the economy. Take the widely quoted example of an upstream irrigation project that is being designed to help farmers increase their agricultural production. The same project, however, could result in decreasing the agricultural production in villages downstream where, as a result, the availability of water may be adversely affected. In financial analysis, or in the accounting of a private entrepreneur, only the direct effects of the upstream irrigation project, i.e., the money value of increased production, will be considered. The private entrepreneur will hardly be concerned with the adverse effects of the project on the downstream villages. On the other hand, for the economy, the sum effects of the project rather than only the direct costs and benefits will be important in determining its profitability. It would take full account of the decrease in agricultural production in downstream villages as well as other negative effects that the project might cause to the economy.

Financial Analysis:	Considers those costs and benefits that are directly attributable to the project in question
Economic Analysis:	Takes note of the total effects of the project, both direct and indirect, in cost-benefit calculations

In its Handbook for Field Directors, OXFAM has given the example of a project that is meant to replace bullocks with tractors. Entitled "The Village-Level Cost-Benefit Budget," it illustrates how the various items of costs (losses) and benefits (gains), direct and indirect, private and social, of a village-level project should be identified and listed. Because of its relevance to the discussion on the differences between the financial and economic analysis, it is reproduced in Example 1.

The economic and financial connotations of profitability are thus quite different from each other. The former looks at the projects from the point of view of their contribution to the economy, while the latter focuses on measuring their financial profitability. Interestingly, although there is a general recognition that the differences

Example 1. Village-Level Cost-Benefit Budget: An Example of a Change from Bullocks to Tractors

Losses	Gains
Revenue Lost	**Extra Revenue**
Custom Work (Bullocks)	Yields Increase Crop Intensity Rises Crop Mixture Changes Acreage Increases Custom Work (Tractor) Alternative Use of Bullock Land
Extra Costs	**Costs Saved**
Fixed Costs of New Machine Operating Costs of New Machines Hired Labour	Bullocks' Concentrated Feed Hired Labour Maintenance of Bullock Equipment
Loss of Cash Income	Gain in Cash Income
Social Loss	**Social Gain**
Polarization of Income Distribution Increase in Unemployment Polarization of Village Structure Dependence on Small Number of Power Units Means Higher Risk of Losing Crops If Machines Break Down	Increase in Leisure and Decrease in Drudgery Increase in Prestige of Some Individuals

Source: Robert Chambers, "Simple is Practical: Approaches and Realities for Project Selection for Poverty-Focused Rural Development", paper presented to the Seminar on the Implications of the Employment and Income Distribution Objectives for Project Appraisal and Identification, Kuwait, 5-6 April, 1977.

between them are pertinent, and should guide the process of project selection, planners have found it extremely difficult to effectively introduce these differences in appraising local development projects. For example, attempts to use the shadow prices or the techniques of assessing direct and indirect effects of projects have met with serious problems of not only the data availability but also of trained manpower who can utilize them in actual practice. The costs of data collection and analysis for economic appraisal of local development projects have been noted as prohibitive, and completely out of proportion to the costs of the projects themselves.

Many authors have viewed the techniques of economic analysis with a great deal of suspicion, and pointed out that aside from adding an aura of sophistication, they have had little or no effect on the actual decisions regarding the candidate projects. Carruthers and Clayton have succinctly expressed this in the following words:

> It is not completely cynical to say that elaborate and superficially impressive appraisal techniques present an aura of spurious accuracy which imbues decision makers with a false sense of confidence when selecting projects. Moreover, the laborious process of shadow pricing, according to the manuals, absorbs an undue amount of skilled effort while the <u>ex-post</u> evaluation reveals that the factors which determine project success or failure are not primarily related to these aspects of planning.[2]

The literature is replete with examples that suggest that changes in the shadow prices have, in actual cases, been made to make projects appear economically profitable. OXFAM's warning in its Handbook for Field Directors is pertinent in this regard: "The danger of using shadow prices is that they may be over- or under-estimated in order to justify projects to which appraiser feels personally committed."[3]

This book also takes the position that the application of shadow pricing and other complex techniques of economic appraisal are not crucial for local development projects. There are other, simple checks, the use of which can provide planners with a fairly sound basis for judgment on whether or not the project's contribution to the local economy will be positive or negative. Simple checks bring decisions into the open, and, as Chambers points out, are less exposed to abuse. Also, unlike social cost-benefit analyses, they are less obscure.[4]

METHODS FOR CALCULATING PROFITABILITY

What methods can be employed to measure profitability? What if the project yields different levels of profits in different years? What kind of an analysis is required for this purpose?

In order to have a fuller appreciation of the analysis involved in calculating profitability, it would be useful to begin with an examination of the various items of costs and benefits of a hypothetical project—such as the one given in Table 5. Table 5 shows the various items of costs that represent the estimated outflows or the payments of the project, as well as the items of benefits that represent the estimated inflows or the receipts of the project.

From Table 5, it should be evident that profits/losses are the difference between the expected value of outputs and the expected value of inputs. The greater the difference, the higher would be the profits/losses. However, the absolute difference between the costs and benefits indicates very little about the earning capacity of this hypothetical project. The difference may be large, but unless it can be interpreted in a way that it gives an idea on the earning capacity of the project, not much significance can be attached to this figure. This is the crux of the profitability analysis. It assesses the earning potential of the resources expected to be invested in the project.

Several methods are in use for calculating profitability, which include:

Simple Methods

(a) Pay-Back Period Method
(b) Simple Rate of Return

Complex or Dynamic Methods

(a) Net Present Value
(b) Benefit-Cost Ratio
(c) Internal Rate of Return

The first two are simple methods, as they rely largely on data for single/representative years. Others may be referred to as complex or dynamical methods, as they take into account the expected inflows and outflows for the entire duration of the project.

Simple Methods

Pay-Back Period. The pay-back period method[5] measures the time within which a project can be expected to recover its total investments through its net profits. In other

TABLE 5
Itemization of costs and benefits for a hypothetical project (in rupees)

	Items	Years						
		1	2	3	4	5	6	7
	A. Expected Costs (value of inputs)							
OUTFLOWS	Capital	250	-	-	-	-	-	-
	Operating:							
	labour		40	40	30	30	30	30
	Raw materials		30	30	30	30	30	30
	Fuel		20	20	30	30	30	30
	Services		20	20	20	20	20	20
	Others		10	10	10	10	10	10
	Interest on loans		25	25	25	25	25	25
	Taxes		5	5	10	15	15	15
	Depreciation		-	-	-	-	-	-
	Sub total	250	150	150	155	160	160	160
	B. Expected Benefits (value of outputs)							
INFLOWS	Sales	-	180	180	210	235	235	235
	Subsidies	-	10	10	-	-	-	-
	Value of assets at the end of the project							
	Sub total	-	190	190	210	235	235	235

words, this method measures the number of years within which the project can accumulate sufficient net profits to cover the amount of its total investment. If the number of years is less than the cut-off period established by the decision maker for recovery of its investments, then the project can be considered safe and acceptable.

The pay-back period method can be used in the following manner:

Step 1. Estimate the total investment likely to be made in the project.

Step 2. Find out the net profits for each year.[6]

Step 3. Deduct from the total investments the net profits of the first year, then of the second, third, and subsequent years until there is no balance left.

Step 4. Count the number of years within which total investment becomes zero. This would represent the pay-back period.

An example showing the use of this method is given in Table 6.

TABLE 6
Application of pay-off period method (in 000 rupees)

Year	Expected costs				Expected total benefits	Net profits or loss	Balance at the end of the year
	Capital	Operat-ing	Interest on loans & taxes	Total			
1	250	-	-	250	-	-250	-250
2	-	120	30	150	190	40	-210
3	-	120	30	150	190	40	-170
4	-	120	35	155	210	55	-115
5	-	120	40	160	235	75	-40
6	-	120	40	160	235	75	+35
7	-	120	40	160	235	75	+110

Source: Table 5.

The application of the pay-back period method, steps 1-4, to the data given in Table 2 would show that it is only in the sixth year that the investments expected to be made in the project could be recovered. The decision that rests with the planners is whether or not the period of repayment of the investments in six years should be considered acceptable or not. If a quicker pay-back is expected, then this project may not be preferred. If, on the other hand, a six-year period for recovery of investments is not considered too long, the project would be considered acceptable.

Simple Rate of Return. The simple rate of return is the ratio of the net profits in a representative year to the total, initial investment. This rate can be computed either on total investments or on equity, depending on whether one wants to know the profitability on the total investments (equity plus loans) or the profitability on only the equity capital.

The simple rate of return can be worked out in the following manner:[7]

Step 1. Estimate the total investment likely to be made on the project (equity and loans)
Step 2. Work out the net profits for any normal year.
Step 3. Divide the net profits by total investment, to arrive at the rate of return.

Thus, the rate of return in the second year will be:
(40+25)/250 = 0.26, or 0.26 x 100 = 26% rate of return

In the fifth year, it will be:
(75+25)/250 = 0.40, or 0.40 x 100 = 40% rate of return

Complex or Dynamic Methods

In addition to the relatively simple methods discussed above, there are others that take into account the entire life cycle of the project for calculating the project's profitability. For the reason that these are able to take into account the variations in the expected outflows and inflows of the project that the project must inevitably face during its life cycle, these are called complex or dynamic methods. The crux of these methods lies in their consideration of time.

Consideration of Time in Project Analysis. It is common knowledge that projects do not earn the same level of profit every year. In some years, profits are high; in others they are low. In many years, it can be expected that the project will earn no profit at all. The question that confronts planners and administrators is how to examine projects that have different time sequence of costs and benefits, and therefore of profits/losses. Table 6 can be taken as the starting point for examining this question.

Table 7 shows the costs and benefits of a hypothetical project over its life cycle of seven years. In the first year, costs are greater then the benefits; in later years, benefits exceed costs.

Two questions arise with respect to Table 7:

TABLE 7
Time sequence of costs and benefits (in 000 rupees)

Year	Items		Difference Between Benefits & Costs
	Costs	Benefits	
1	250	-	-250
2	150	190	+40
3	150	190	+40
4	155	210	+55
5	160	235	+75
6	160	235	+75
7	160	235	+75
Total	1,185	1,295	110

1. How should the flow or the stream of costs and benefits be reduced to a comparable figure? It should be obvious that the overall profitability of this, or any other project, cannot be assessed on a year-to-year basis. Expected profits of this project as shown in the table vary between years. Also, if a year-to-year assessment is attempted, it will be a time-consuming exercise, and may not be able to give any definite conclusion as to its profitability. So, the task for the planners is to reduce the flows into a single figure that can indicate the earning capacity or the profitability of the project in question. How should this be done?
2. How should the "value" of money over time be treated? Should the value of Rs.75,000 that is likely to be the level of net profits in the fourth year of the project (see Table 3) be taken at its face value, or be adjusted to take note of the fall in the value of money from inflation as well as the uncertainty that is implicit in any consideration of the "future." What is the method by which the problem of time can be resolved?

The method of dealing with the flows of costs and benefits over time in project analysis is called time-discounting. This is a method of reducing to a comparable base the costs and benefits of a project that accrue at different intervals. The underlying thesis in this concept is that the value of money is different at different points of time; for instance, $1,000 or Rs.5,000 received today is not of equal worth to a similar amount ten years from now. In other words, costs which have to be paid in the distant future have, at present, a lower significance or value than those to be paid now. Similarly, the benefits which accrue from a project now are of a greater value than those accruing later. Calculation of the present value of costs and benefits involves the use of a discount factor, which is nothing but a rate at which the future is to be discounted. Discount rate represents the present value of the future.

To repeat: the crux of time-discounting is that the value of money is different at different points in time. One thousand rupees received today cannot be equal in worth to Rs.1,000 received in one year's time. Its value will be lower than Rs.1,000. Inflation and uncertainty reduce the value of money over time.

How can the time-discounting method be applied to projects?

Consider the last column in Table 3, which shows the difference between the costs and benefits of the project for the duration of its expected life. Further assume that the task of the planner is to find out the present values of the amounts shown in the last column at an 8 percent rate of discount. The planner has chosen an 8 percent rate of discount, as he thinks that the value of money would, in the next few years, depreciate at roughly this rate.

In order to explain the application of the time-discounting method, it is useful to briefly recall the manner in which compound interests are calculated. Assume that there is an amount of $100 that is expected to earn interest at 8 percent per annum. In one year, the amount of $100 will increase at this rate to $108.00 [$=100(1+(8/100))$]; in two years, this amount will be $116.60 [$=\{100(1+(8/100))\}^2$], and in three years the amount will increase to $125.90 [$=\{100(1+(8/100))\}^3$], and so on. The formula that is used is conveniently written as:

$$F = P(1+r)^n$$

where F = future worth
P = present worth
r = rate of interest
n = number of years

or

Future worth (F)	$= P(1 + r)$	----------	Year (1)
	$= P(1 + r)^2$	----------	Year (2)
	$= P(1 + r)^3$	----------	Year (3)
	$= \ldots\ldots$		
	$= P(1 + r)^n$	----------	Year (n)

It can also be shown graphically:

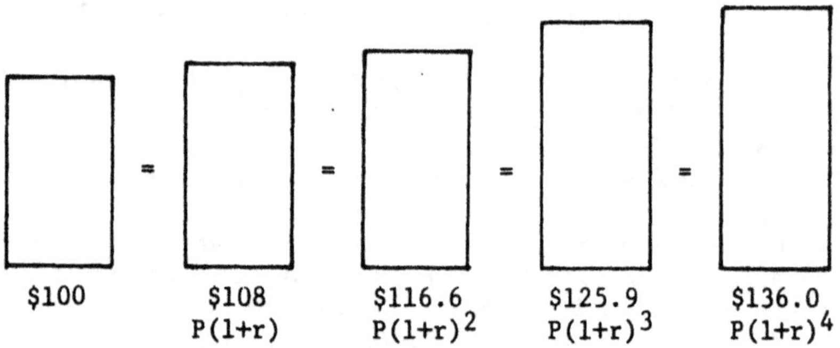

Compounding is nothing other than finding out the future worth of the present at a given rate of interest. Discounting is just the reverse of compounding. In discounting, the expected future values are given and their present values have to be determined at a given discount rate. This involves using the inverse of the compounding formula:

$$P = F \times 1/(1+r)^n$$

or

$$\text{Present worth (P)} = F \times \frac{1}{(1+r)} \quad \text{------------} \quad \text{Year (1)}$$

$$= F \times \frac{1}{(1+r)^2} \quad \text{------------} \quad \text{Year (2)}$$

$$= F \times \frac{1}{(1+r)^3} \quad \text{------------} \quad \text{Year (3)}$$

$$= \ldots\ldots$$

$$= F \times \frac{1}{(1+r)^n} \quad \text{------------} \quad \text{Year (n)}$$

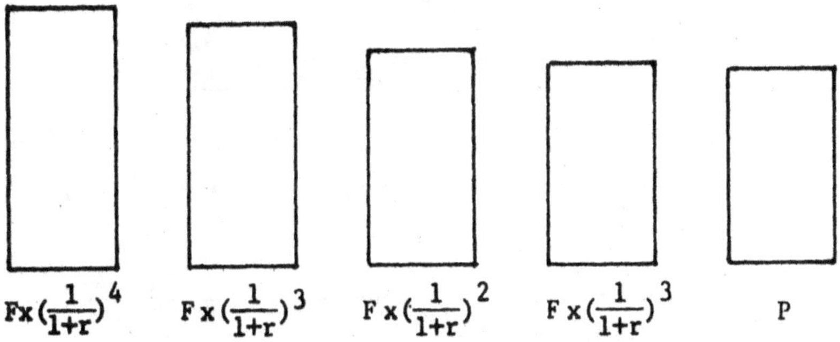

Let us use the figures given in Table 8 as an example to show how time-discounting can be used to find out the present worth of the future values.

TABLE 8
Use of time-discounting

Year	Values ($)	Discount Rate (11%)	Present Worth ($)
0	100	1.00	
1	120		
2	130		
3	140		
4	150		
Total	640		

Calculation of the present worth of the values given in column 2 at 11 percent discount rate would involve:

1. Finding out the present worth of 1 at 11 percent discount rates for years 1 to 4, which would be:[8]

$$= 1 \times \left(\frac{1}{1+11\%}\right) \text{ ------------------- Year (1)}$$

$$= 1 \times (0.90) \qquad = 0.90$$

$$= 1 \times \left(\frac{1}{1+11\%}\right)^2 \text{ ------------------- Year (2)}$$

$$= 1 \times 0.81 \qquad = 0.81$$

$$= 1 \times \left(\frac{1}{1+11\%}\right)^3 \text{ ------------------- Year (3)}$$

$$= 1 \times 0.73 \qquad = 0.73$$

$$= 1 \times \left(\frac{1}{1+11\%}\right)^4 \text{ ------------------- Year (4)}$$

$$= 1 \times 0.66 \qquad = 0.66$$

2. Multiplying the present worth of 1 for years 1 to 4 to the values given in column 2 for the respective years:

100 x 1.00	=	100.0
120 x 0.90	=	108.0
130 x 0.81	=	105.3
140 x 0.73	=	102.2
150 x 0.66	=	99.0

3. Adding the present worth of the values as worked out in step 2 to arrive at the total present worth of \$640. This is \$514.50.

The example shows that the present worth of \$640 (accruing in the manner as shown above) at 11 percent discount rate is \$514.50. It means that when an amount is discounted back to the present, its present worth is always less than its future worth. It also means that the higher the discount rate, the lower would be its present value.

Time-discounting is the foundation for all dynamic methods used for calculating the "profitability" of the projects. It is thus important for planners to be acquainted not only with the mechanics of discounting, but also with what the different discount rates indicate, and when, and under what conditions, planners should use higher or lower discount rates. When the future carries greater risk and uncertainty, and the fear of inflation or deteriorating economic situations, a higher discount rate is generally used. Conversely, a lower discount rate would suffice when the economic and social situations are stable, and no dramatic changes are expected to take place in the future.

It should be pointed out that the decision on what discount rate should be used for appraising projects is made at the central government's level, and rarely are local levels involved in such decisions. However, an understanding of what the different rates indicate helps local-level planners in placing the projects in a proper perspective. The discussion on the use of the complex methods of project appraisal that follows also has to be viewed in this context.[9]

Three methods are discussed here. These are (1) net present value, (2) benefit-cost ratio, and (3) internal rate of return. Other methods that are in use are variants of the above and are therefore left out of discussion in this book.

In order to be able to fully grasp the significance of these methods, it is useful to revert to the example of a local situation where, let it be assumed, an entrepreneur has submitted to the local industries officer a project proposing the establishment of a small-scale manufacturing unit. The proposal contains the necessary details: a description of the aims, objectives, and activities, the _raison d'etre_ of the project, and an estimate of the various items of costs and benefits. The project is estimated to have a life of eight years after which major replacement of machinery and equipment would be required. The entrepreneur is seeking a loan from the local industries department for the establishment of this manufacturing unit. The task of the local industries officer in such a situation is to make an assessment as to whether or not the project has a sound base, and whether or not the project, if established, would be profitable. For him to agree to the loan, it is crucial that he knows about the project's earning capacity and internal strength.

The net present value (NPV), the benefit-cost ratio, and the internal rate of return (IRR) and their variants are methods that enable planners in gauging the earning capacity and strengths of the projects under consideration.

Net Present Value Method. The net present value is defined as the value arrived at by deducting the costs from the benefits of a project, discounted over its anticipated life span. In other words, the NPV is the difference between the discounted costs (cash outflows) and the discounted benefits (cash inflows). It measures the net cash flows of a project. In case the difference is positive, the project is *prima facie* considered safe. When a number of projects are under consideration, those with higher NPVs are to be generally preferred over those with lower NPVs.

> Net present value = [Discounted cash inflows
> - Discounted cash outflows]

The net present value method can be used by taking the following steps (Table 9):[10]

Step 1. Estimate the cash inflows and outflows on a year-to-year basis.
Step 2. Work out the net cash flows for individual years
Step 3. Find out for individual years the discount value of 1 at the given discount rate
Step 4. Multiply the net cash flows for each year by the corresponding discount factor
Step 5. Add up the present values

It can be seen from the example in Table 9 that at a 12 percent rate of discount the net present values of the project are negative (-15.1). The project, therefore, cannot be accepted. If, however, a lower discount rate is used, say 8 percent, the net values of the project would turn positive, and the project may gain acceptability. The net values at 8 percent discount rate are shown in Table 10.

TABLE 9
Computing the net present values (1) (in Rs.1,000)

Year	Costs (Outflows)	Benefits (Inflows)	Benefits-Costs (Net Cash Flows)	Values of 1 at 12% Discount Rate	Discounted Net Cash Flows
	(Step 1)		(Step 2)	(Step 3)	(Step 4)
0	250	-	-250	1.00	-250
1	150	190	40	0.892	35.7
2	150	190	40	0.797	31.9
3	155	210	55	0.712	39.2
4	160	235	75	0.635	47.6
5	160	235	75	0.567	42.5
6	160	235	75	0.507	38.0
Total	1,185	1,295			-15.1 (Step 5)

Source: Table 5.

TABLE 10
Computing the Net Present Values (2) (in Rs.1,000)

Year	Benefits-Costs (Net Cash Flows)	Values of 1 at 8% Discount Rate	Discounted Net Cash Flows
	(Step 2)*	(Step 3)	(Step 4)
0	-250	1.00	-250
1	40	0.92	37.2
2	40	0.86	34.4
3	55	0.79	43.5
4	75	0.74	54.8
5	75	0.68	51.0
6	75	0.63	47.2
Total			+18.1 (Step 5)

*Source: Table 9.

<u>Benefit-Cost</u> <u>Ratio</u>. The benefit-cost ratio is a ratio calculated by dividing the sum of discounted benefits by discounted costs. Steps for calculating the benefit-cost ratio are:[11]

$$\text{Benefit-Cost Ratio} = \frac{\text{Sum of Discounted Benefits}}{\text{Sum of Discounted Costs}}$$

Step 1. Estimate the cash inflows and outflows on a year-to-year basis

Step 2. Find out for individual years the discount value of 1 at the given discount rate

Step 3. Multiply the cash inflows and cash outflows for each year by the corresponding discount factor

Step 4. Add up the discounted values of cash inflows and outflows separately

Step 5. Divide the discounted values of cash inflows by cash outflows to obtain the benefit-cost ratio

The computation of benefit-cost ratio is shown in Table 11.

TABLE 11
Computing the benefit-cost ratio

Year	Costs (Outflows)	Benefits (Inflows)	Discount Factor at 8%	Discounted Values	
				Costs	Benefits
	(Step 1)		(Step 2)	(Steps 3 & 4)	
0	250	-	1.000	250	-
1	150	190	.93	139.5	176.7
2	150	190	.86	129.0	163.4
3	155	210	.76	122.4	165.9
4	160	235	.73	116.8	171.6
5	160	235	.68	108.8	159.8
6	160	235	.63	100.8	148.0
Total				967.3	985.4

Step 5: 985.4/967.3 = 1.018

The benefit-cost ratio in the above example is greater than 1, indicating that the sum of the discounted benefits is greater than the sum of the discounted costs. If the ratio had been less than 1, as indeed it is at 12 percent discount rate, it would not be advisable to accept the project. Also, as in the case of the NPV, the higher the benefit-cost ratio of a project, the better it is in terms of profitability.

Internal Rate of Return. The internal rate of return is a rate of discount at which the net present values of a project are zero. Or, expressed differently, it is a rate at which the discounted costs and discounted benefits become equal. The rate represents the "effective interest earned on the investment in the project."[12] In the words of Gittinger, it "is the maximum interest that a project could pay for the resources used if the project is to recover its investment and operating costs and still breakeven."[13]

Internal Rate of Return =	A rate at which the discounted costs are equal to discounted benefits

Unlike the two other methods discussed earlier where the present values or the benefit-cost ratios are calculated on the basis of the given discount rates, in the case of the internal rate of return, a rate at which the discounted costs would become equal to discounted benefits has to be found out. The higher the IRR, the stronger is the project.

The calculation of the internal rate of return involves the following steps:[14]

Step 1. Estimate the cash inflows and cash outflows on a year-to-year basis

Step 2. Work out the net cash flows for individual years

Step 3. Select any random discount rate and compute the net present values

Step 4. If the NPV thus arrived at is positive, then select a higher discount rate at which the NPV may come close to zero. If, however, the NPV is negative, then select a lower discount rate at which the NPV may come close to zero.

Step 5. Repeat the exercise until a discount rate that reduces the net present values to zero is found

The entire exercise of finding out the internal rate of return involves trial and error. As Gittinger writes:

> Except by lucky accident, one cannot simply choose that discount rate which will make the incremental net benefit stream equal to zero. . . . Unhappily, there is no formula for finding the internal rate of return. We are forced to resort to a systematic procedure of trial and error to find that discount rate which will make the net present worth of the incremental net benefit stream equal zero.[15]

An example using the figures given in Table 5 may once again be taken to illustrate the computation of the internal rate of return.

TABLE 12
Computing the internal rate of return (1)

Year	Costs (Cash Outflows)	Benefits (Cash Inflows)	Net Cash Flows	Net Present Values Discounted		
				8%		12%
	(Step 1)		(Step 2)	(Step 3)		(Step 4)
0	250		-250	-250		-250
1	150	190	40	37.2		35.7
2	150	190	40	34.4		31.9
3	155	210	55	43.5		39.2
4	160	235	75	54.8		47.6
5	160	235	75	51.0		42.5
6	160	235	75	47.2		38.0
Total				18.1		-15.1

In this example, the initial discounting of the net cash flows (Step 3) has been done at 8 percent, which gives a positive net present value of 18.1. Step 4, that is, discounting at 12 percent, turns the net values to a negative figure of 15.1, suggesting that the rate at which the discounted net values would turn zero must lie somewhere between 8 and 12 percent.

Repeating the exercise with 9, 10, and 11 percent gives values that are very close to zero. The rate at which the discounted costs equal discounted benefits comes to 10.1 percent.[16] These values are given in Table 13.

TABLE 13
Computing the internal rate of return (2) (net cash flows at different discount rates)

Year	Net Cash Flows	Net Present Values Discounted at							
		9%		10%		11%		10.1%	
0	-250	1.00	-250	1.00	-250	1.00	-250	1.00	-250
1	40	0.92	36.8	0.91	36.4	0.90	36.0	0.91	36.4
2	40	0.84	33.6	0.83	33.2	0.81	32.4	0.82	32.8
3	55	0.77	42.4	0.75	41.3	0.73	40.2	0.75	41.3
4	75	0.71	53.2	0.68	51.0	0.66	49.5	0.68	51.0
5	75	0.65	48.8	0.62	46.5	0.59	44.3	0.62	46.5
6	75	0.60	45.0	0.56	42.0	0.53	39.8	0.56	42.0
Total Net Values			9.8		0.4		-7.8		0.0

It would thus be noted that the calculation of the internal rate of return requires repetitive computations, and is often taxing. Gittinger's observations in this behalf are relevant to be reproduced here.

> Just where does the real internal rate of return lie? We could find out by successfully narrowing down our limits until finally we find the discount rate that will make the sum exactly zero, but this would require much repetitive computation and the use of fractional discount factors for which no tables exist (as in the above example).[17]

An alternative to the use of repetitive computations is "interpolation," which is a technique of finding the intermediate values between any two figures, or any two discount rates in the present context. The equation for interpolation is as follows:[18]

$$\text{Internal rate of return} = \text{Lower discount rate} + \left(\begin{array}{c}\text{Difference}\\ \text{between the}\\ \text{discount rates}\end{array}\right)\left(\frac{\text{Net present value at the lower discount rate}}{\begin{array}{c}\text{Sum of the net present values}\\ \text{at the two discount rates}\\ \text{(ignore sign)}\end{array}}\right)$$

or

$$\begin{aligned}\text{Internal rate of return} &= 8 + (12-8)\frac{18.1}{(18.1) - (-15.1)} && \text{------ (1)}\\ &= 8 + (4)\frac{18.1}{33.2} && \text{------ (2)}\\ &= 8 + (4)(.54) && \text{------ (3)}\\ &= 8 + 2.1 && \text{------ (4)}\\ &= 10.1 \text{ rate of discount}\end{aligned}$$

This is the way in which the internal rate of return is calculated. As mentioned earlier, projects with higher IRRs are considered financially safer and stronger. Evidently, it would be inadvisable to accept projects whose IRRs are lower than the prevailing lending or borrowing interest rates in the capital market of the country.

It should be mentioned that the internal rate of return is the most widely used method for appraising development projects. Most international and bilateral aid agencies rely on this method as a guide to decisions on projects in question, of course, among several other considerations. The main advantage of the IRR is that it is less subject to maneuvering than either the net present value or the benefit-cost ratio methods. In their cases, almost everything about the projects depends on the discount rates: by changing the discount rates, results as desired by the planners or administrators can be obtained. This is not possible to be done in the case of the internal rate of return where, if favorable results were to be sought on a particular project, the entire streams of costs and benefits of the project will need to be changed.

Two points regarding the methods explained above must be stressed here. The first point refers to the choice between the various methods: which of them is more effective and appropriate to be used for local-level development projects, and able to provide planners with a reasonably sound indication on the profitability of the projects in question? Is a particular method superior to another? This question cannot be answered in any definitive manner. At the same time, it is true that the profitability of a project could vary with the method to be employed. In fact, the literature on project analysis has numerous examples, which shows that the profitability of a project could substantially change with the use of the one or the other method. This is true particularly for projects that are expected to encounter variations in the cash flows during their life cycle. In such situations, it would seem appropriate to use the various methods in conjunction with each other. This would provide planners with the confidence necessary for project selection. Format 9 is an indicative format for summarizing the results of the profitability analysis. This format could also be used for comparing the profitability of various candidate projects in order to determine which of them is more profitable.

Format 9. Indicative Format for Comparing the Results of Profitability Analysis

Candidate Projects	Pay-Back Period (Number of Years)	Simple Rate of Return (in %)	Net Present Value	Benefit: Cost Ratio	Internal Rate of Return (in %)
A					
B					
C					
D					
Decision Maker's Norms					

The second point to be stressed here is that the methods for calculating profitability are the same whether one is attempting a financial or an economic analysis. However, in the latter case, several changes have to be made in the itemization of the project's costs and benefits as well as in their valuation. The economic analysis has to be made in terms of the opportunity costs to the economy than the actual financial payments or receipts.[19] These aspects have already been explained in the earlier part of this chapter.

As a final remark on these methods, it should be added that each one of them has its own problem of, as Bendavid-Val says, "what to count." His related observations on the subject are also instructive to be noted in dealing with these methods:

> The more the perspective on costs and benefits is broadened, the more difficult the counting problem becomes. The easiest case is that in which the project is viewed as a single project-making enterprise. But economic development projects seldom can be viewed so simply. Because the notion of cost-benefit analysis derives from business planning, and because what is good for a single private business may be bad for private enterprise or the economy collectively, there are frequently situations in which the appropriateness of the conventional cost-benefit analysis approach is arguable. Equally frequent are situations in which the interpretation of the results of a cost-benefit analysis is entirely in dispute.[20]

APPRAISAL OF INDIRECTLY PRODUCTIVE AND PROMOTIONAL PROJECTS

Let us turn our attention to the third and final question listed at the beginning of this chapter: How should the profitability of projects such as the schools, health centers, rural roads, sites and services, low-income group housing, marketplaces and the like be measured? How do we know that the investments in such projects would be effective, and be able to achieve the goals and objectives of the sectors to which such projects might belong? Evidently, the question is complex because of the nature of the benefits of such projects, which are not amenable to easy measurement in money or quantitative terms. The benefits of such projects are described, in most cases, in qualitative terms, and therefore are subject to varying interpretation by planners and administrators. Also, because of the qualitative nature, these cannot be weighed against the costs of the projects--in a manner similar to projects, e.g., in the agricultural or industrial sectors. No breakthrough has occurred in developing a methodology for appraising such projects, nor does one appear to be in sight even though these projects remain the most direct concern of the governments and account for a sizable proportion of their investments.

In order to fully appreciate the nature of the problem involved in appraising them, a few examples of such projects may be taken at the very outset. Consider the costs and benefits of a rural roads improvement project. The cost side would list the usual items, and include the costs of, for example, the surveying and drafting equipment; machines and tools such as road graders, road rollers, concrete mixers; soils, tar, and other materials; utility trucks with water sprinklers; fuel; some office equipment and supplies; and the costs of supervisory staff; labor; etc. Likewise, several items would be shown on the benefits side, too. There would be, first of all, the savings on the operating costs of the vehicles. Because of the improved roads, the operating costs of the vehicles would obviously be lower. It would be shown that the roads project would provide the local population with opportunities to negotiate for higher prices for their farm products. The local farmers would also be able to obtain agricultural inputs at lower costs. Because of the road, it would be easier to extend better farming techniques into the area, which would lead to improved agricultural productivity and better incomes. If these are put in the form of a balance sheet, the project's costs and benefits would appear as in Example 2.

Or, take the case of the "Paving the Gravel Road" project at the end of this chapter. What are the outputs/benefits of this project? A number of benefits can be identified. First, the maintenance and operating costs of vehicles likely to pass through this road will decline as a result of the project. If maintenance of the gravel road costs TK2.48/km, it may cost TK1.58/km for a paved road. This is a benefit that can be easily measured. Second, if this project is finally accepted, then the gravel road that would then have been paved will not be required to be maintained, and the maintenance costs of the gravel road will be avoided. This also is a benefit that can be accounted for in the analysis. Third, the paved road would accelerate the movement of goods and services and result in faster economic growth. Although it may be possible to estimate the growth in traffic based on either past trends or new assumptions,

Example 2. An Indicative Balance Sheet of Costs and Benefits of a Rural Roads Improvement Project

Costs	Benefits
1. Machinery, Equipment and Tools	
Surveying & drafting equipment	1. Savings on the operating costs of the vehicles
Road graders & rollers	2. Provision of economical transportation to the local area
Concrete mixers	
2. Materials	3. Provide local population with opportunities to negotiate for higher prices for their products
Soils	
Tar	
Concrete	
Others	4. Be able to obtain agricultural inputs at lower costs
3. Fuel	5. Easy transferability of better farming techniques
Utility trucks with water sprinklers	
4. Office Equipment & Supplies	
5. Supervisory Staff & Labour	

its impact on economic growth will be difficult to assess. This is perhaps the most significant benefit that would emerge from the road, but one that may not be possible to measure.

Consider another project, in the health sector. What kinds of benefits would accrue from a health project that includes, let us assume, a component for child care. Surely, the most important benefit that can be expected of such a project is the reduction in the number of sick days, resulting in increased productivity and income for the local population. Some authors have estimated that if a health project, through its dispensation, is able to add for every member of its working population just one day in a year to the total number of working days, the project's costs would be more than covered by the generation of additional incomes. There are many other benefits of such a project, a few of which are listed in Example 3.

Example 3. Costs and Benefits of a Health Project

Costs	Benefits
1. Construction of the health centre & related facilities 2. Medical & professional equipment 3. Equipment for training of paramedics 4. Vehicles & fuel 5. Medicines 6. Project administration & supervision	1. Reduce the number of sick days & thereby contribute to increased productivity & incomes 2. Improved child care would reduce infant mortality, & promote acceptance of family planning 3. Raise the quality & productive capacity of the future workforce 4. Assist the government in achieving its objectives of improving health & nutritional standards 5. Provision of health and health-related services to __ per cent of the local population

Take the example of a school project. The purpose of a school project will be to create facilities for school-going age children so that they can:

1. Obtain education
2. Be prepared to enter the labor force with greater confidence
3. Improve opportunities for gainful employment
4. Develop skills to better communicate in the society
5. Contribute more to raising the area's living standards, incomes, and quality of life

And so on. The benefits of a school project are numerous, but only a few of them are measurable. Another interesting project in this category, which has assumed some degree of importance in many countries, is about the involvement of women and other bypassed groups in the development process. It has been contended that if conscious efforts are made to involve such groups in the process of economic and social development, the overall pace of development would be considerably accelerated. As in the case of other projects mentioned earlier, it is extremely difficult to list the net gains of such a project. Planners, administrators, and people's representatives see the desirability of such projects, but when they are asked to weigh their advantages in relation to the expected costs, they find it difficult to do so.

How then should such projects be appraised? What indicators should be used for planners to prioritize them?

The literature on project analysis has suggested that there are two ways in which projects in this category could be appraised. One is what has been called the goal-achievement method; the second is referred to as the cost-effective method. The purpose of the goal-achievement method is to find out whether or not the projects under consideration would help in the achievement of the goals that may have been set for the development of the local area, or the goals of the sectors/subsectors to which the projects might belong. If the application of this method can establish that the projects would, in fact, contribute to the goals, then they deserve to be accorded a high priority. The candidate projects can also be ranked according to the degree to which they might contribute to the achievement of the various goals.

The cost-effective method, as the name suggests, aims at ascertaining the effectiveness of the costs or investments expected to be made in the projects under consideration. Put in other words, this is a method of finding out whether or not the projects would effectively use the proposed investments, and whether or not they would maximize the expected benefits per unit of proposed investments. Both methods imply that there is no way other than the projects selected in this manner that the goals for the concerned area can be achieved, and the effectiveness of the investments maximized.

For the application of the goal-achievement method, it is instructive to refer to a recent article written by Leinbach and Gromley[21] in which they explain how they utilized a set of "nineteen goals" in the selection of rural road projects in the Indonesian Rural Works Programme.[22] According to the article, a set of nineteen variables were initially selected for inclusion in the goal-programming model. Variables were selected with specific objectives in mind. Thus, for example, variable 2 (see Example 4) stipulates that a minimum number of people must be served per project, and that an aggregate, combined population threshold level across all projects must, as well, be achieved (variable 1). "In order to expand food production projects should serve land that is now agriculturally productive but will become more so with improved access" (variable 3).

Example 4. Rural Roads Project: Selected Variables

1. Total Population
2. Threshold Population
3. Total Agricultural Land
4. Potential Agricultural Land
5. Resource Conversion Requirement
6. Higher Order Connection
7. Internal Access
8. Integrated Development Scheme
9. Daily Market Distance
10. Facilities Served
11. Road Length
12. Bridge Costs
13. Estate Land
14. Off Season Unemployment
15. Competing Road
16. Distance to Surface Materials
17. Projects Cost Total
18. Self Help Level
19. Projects Constructed

The second step in the process was to define the attainment or the goal level with respect to each criterion, and to rank them in order of priority. The nineteen criteria were grouped into six separate priority levels and assigned specific attainment levels, as shown in Table 14. "The most important objectives are grouped together at the P_0 priority level; goals in the P_1 priority level are less important than those in P_0 while goals with a P_5 ranking are considered to be the least important in the model."[23] Solution is then sought, and thirteen out of the twenty potential East Javan road projects are chosen for implementation.[24]

TABLE 14
Attainment levels and goal priorities: Basic model

Priority Level	Criteria	Attainment Level
P_0	1. Minimum total population served	55,000 people
P_0	11. Maximum road length per project	8 kms
P_0	12. Maximum total bridge costs	30 million Rs.
P_0	14. Minimum off season unemployment level per project	35% unemployed
P_0	15. Maximum Number of competing roads	3 roads
P_0	17. Maximum total project costs	260 million Rs.
P_1	19. Minimum number of projects funded	12 projects
P_2	2. Threshold population served per project	2,000 people
P_2	3. Minimum total agricultural land served	2,250 he
P_3	8. Minimum number of projects that are part of an integrated development scheme	1 project
P_3	10. Minimum number of facilities served	15 facilities
P_3	16. Maximum distance to surfacing materials per project	30 kms
P_3	18. Minimum percentage of villages that have demonstrated adequate self-help records per project	50%
P_4	4. Minimum amount of potential agricultural land to be converted	650 he
P_4	6. Minimum number of projects that link to a higher order road	5 projects
P_4	7. Minimum number of projects that improve internal accessibility	7 projects
P_4	9. Maximum distance to a daily market per project	12 kms
P_5	5. Maximum man days available for land conversion	200 man days
P_5	13. Maximum amount of estate land included within project areas	100 he

What the above example suggests is that if the planners decide to use the goal-achievement method for appraising and prioritizing projects, they would be required to take at least the following steps:[25]

Step 1. Define goals
Step 2. Set minimum achievement levels for each goal
Step 3. Prioritize goals
Step 4. Determine which projects satisfy which goals

Format 10 incorporates these steps.

The term "cost-effective" is not easy to define; indeed, there are few authors who have attempted to define the term in any precise manner. In simple words, what it means is that the resources should be allocated for those projects that are likely to result in the largest number of benefits or units of outputs. The less the cost of any means to achieve a given goal, the more cost-effective it is. Some authors have defined it as "benefit-cost analysis without monetary valuation of programme outputs."[26]

At least three steps are required in order to apply the cost-effectiveness criterion to the candidate projects:

Step 1. Identification of quantifiable and nonquantifiable outputs or benefits
Step 2. Estimation of the monetary resources expected to be put in
Step 3. Computation of the cost-effectiveness ratio

or

$$\text{C : E Ratio} = \frac{\text{Quantifiable and nonquantifiable outputs}}{\text{Monetary costs}}$$

$$= \frac{\text{Quantifiable and nonquantifiable outputs}}{\text{Per unit of monetary costs}}$$

Those projects that are expected to yield higher outputs per unit of monetary costs would evidently be preferable over others.

Having described the use of the goal-achievement and cost-effectiveness methods, it should be mentioned that the use of neither of the two methods is easy at local levels. Both methods require manpower trained specifically in the application of these methods, which, at present, are unavailable in most developing countries. For instance, the goal-programming is derived from management sciences. For

Format 10. Using the Goal-Achievement Method at Local Levels

Projects by Sectors/ Subsectors	Goals with Minimum Achievement Levels														
	1			2			3			4			5		
	Degree of Satisfaction														
	High	Medium	Low	High	Medium	Low	High	Medium	Low	High	Medium	Low	High	Medium	Low
Education															
1															
2															
3															
Health															
1															
2															
3															
Housing															
1															
2															
3															
Involvement of the bypassed groups in the development process															
1															
2															
3															

untrained manpower, it would be neither easy to identify "goals" nor fix the "achievement or attainment levels." Also, the methods themselves are vulnerable.

As an alternative to these complicated methods, it is considered adequate at local levels to use a set of simple "output indicators" for ensuring that the resources will be committed for the right kinds of projects, and that the selected projects would be the most cost-effective options. In Bangladesh, for instance, the Ministry of Local Government and Rural Development has proposed a set of "preference criteria" for selection of roads, bridges, culverts, rehabilitation of derelict tanks, markets, godowns, and similar projects. According to the proposal, preference should be given to projects that fulfill, among others, the following conditions:

1. Projects with a higher labor intensity
2. Projects that have a direct positive impact on productive output
3. Projects that are likely to create more employment for disadvantaged groups
4. Projects that are expected to generate long-term employment
5. Projects that will generate production for export purposes
6. Projects that will generate income for the local bodies to make them more self-reliant

Similar indicators are possible to be developed for other categories of projects. A set of illustrative indicators is given in Example 5.

What does the discussion on profitability made in this chapter add up to? How would the planners at the local levels use this information for purposes of project selection?

Three observations would sum up the responses to these questions:

1. This chapter has demonstrated how, and by what methods, planners can calculate the profitability of the candidate projects. It has shown how data on costs and benefits given in Block E of Format 7 in Chapter 2 should be treated for purposes of financial and economic analysis, and how the project's costs and benefits should be compared.
2. This chapter has shown how projects whose benefits or outputs are not measureable in quantitative

Example 5. Illustrative List of Output Indicators

Type of Project	Illustrative Indicators
Primary School	1. Number of students likely to attend the school/per unit of investment costs 2. Durable employment expected to be generated by the project/per unit of investment costs
Health Centre	1. Number of patients likely to take advantage of the health centre/per unit of investment costs 2. Durable employment expected to be generated by the project/per unit of investment costs
Urban Development	1. Number of squatters likely to be resettled/per unit of investment costs 2. Number of people likely to benefit from water supply scheme under the urban development project/per unit of investment costs
Involvement of Women in the Development Process	1. Number of women likely to be covered by the project/per unit of investment costs 2. Expected increase in earnings of the participant women/per unit of investment costs

terms should be appraised. What methods or indicators should be used to ascertain the achievement levels of the projects in relation to the goals?

3. This chapter has added the results of the profitability analysis to the information contained in the "prefeasibility briefs," giving the planners and decision makers additional data to decide whether to abandon the projects or to carry them forward for further analysis and consideration.

Profitability analysis remains the single most important test for all development projects.

NOTES

1. Shadow price of the labor would be equal to the market price multiplied by the factor by which it stands overpriced (market price multiplied by the adjustment factor). The shadow price of foreign exchange would likewise be equal to the market price multiplied by the factor by which it stands underpriced (market price multiplied by the adjustment factor).

2. I. D. Carruthers and E. S. Clayton, "Ex-Post Evaluation of Agricultural Projects--Its Implication for Planning," quoted in Robert Chambers, "Simple is Practical: Approaches and Realities for Project Selection for Poverty-Focused Rural Development," paper presented at the Seminar on the Implications of the Employment and Income Distribution Objectives for Project Appraisal and Identification, Kuwait, 5-6 April 1977, p. 11.

3. Robert Chambers, ibid., p. 8.

4. Robert Chambers, ibid., p. 14.

Simple procedures being decisions into the open...... One reason why cost-benefit analysis is so exposed to abuse is that it is obscure. It is easy, and is known to be easy, to adjust discount rates and shadow prices to produce a wide range of results. Rationality may be best defined through selection procedures which can easily be understood by a noneconomist layman.

5. Pay-back method can be expressed as follows:

$$I = \sum_{t=0}^{P} Ft$$

where: I = Investment
P = Pay-back period
F = Annual net profits in t^{th} year

6. Net profits =
Income + (Operating cost + Taxes) + Interest

7. The formula for calculating the simple rate of return is:

$$\text{Simple rate of return} = \frac{\text{Net profits + Interest}}{\text{Initial investment}}$$

or

$$R = \frac{F + y}{I}$$

where: R = Rate of return
F = Net profits (see Note 6)
y = Interest
I = Initial investment

8. The present worth of 1 at various discount rates is given in what are called the Discount Tables. One set of Discount Tables is shown on the following page. The present worth of 1 at 11 percent discount rate for years 1 to 20 can, for instance, be seen in the relevant column.

An alternative to using the Discount Tables is a calculator. Most calculators have keys that can easily find discounted values. The relevant steps for finding the discounted values by using a calculator of the type depicted would be:

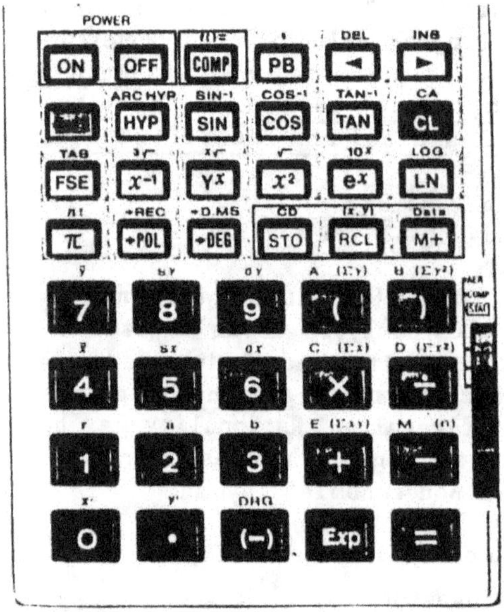

a. Enter the constant: In the example for an 11 percent discount rate, the constant is 1/(1+11%) or 1/(1+.11). So, first enter 1, and divide it by 1.11, and then turn the result (0.9009009) into a constant by pressing the multiplication sign twice.

b. Press the "=" key in order to get the discounted value of 1 for year 2 (0.811622433).

c. Press the "=" key again in order to get the discounted value of 1 for year 3 (0.731191381), and keep repeating for the number of years the discounted values are required.

9. Planners must resist the temptation of using lower discount rates in appraising projects. Projects could appear very promising when, in fact, they may not be so.

10.

$$NPV = B + \left(\frac{B_1}{(1+r)} + \frac{B_2}{(1+r)^2} + \dots \frac{B_n}{(1+r)^n}\right) - C + \left(\frac{C_1}{(1+r)} + \frac{C_2}{(1+r)^2} + \dots \frac{C_n}{(1+r)^n}\right)$$

Present Values of 1 at Various Discount Rates

Year	2 %	3 %	4 %	5 %	5½ %	6 %	6½ %	7 %	7½ %	8 %	8½ %	9 %	9½ %	10 %	11 %	12 %	13 %	14 %	15 %	16 %	18 %	20 %	25 %	30 %
1	0.980	0.971	0.962	0.952	0.948	0.943	0.939	0.935	0.930	0.926	0.922	0.917	0.913	0.909	0.901	0.893	0.885	0.877	0.870	0.862	0.847	0.833	0.800	0.769
2	0.961	0.943	0.925	0.907	0.898	0.890	0.882	0.873	0.865	0.857	0.849	0.842	0.834	0.826	0.812	0.797	0.783	0.769	0.756	0.743	0.718	0.694	0.640	0.592
3	0.942	0.915	0.889	0.864	0.852	0.840	0.828	0.816	0.805	0.794	0.783	0.772	0.762	0.751	0.731	0.712	0.693	0.675	0.658	0.641	0.609	0.579	0.512	0.455
4	0.924	0.888	0.855	0.823	0.807	0.792	0.777	0.763	0.749	0.735	0.722	0.708	0.696	0.683	0.659	0.636	0.613	0.592	0.572	0.552	0.516	0.482	0.410	0.350
5	0.906	0.863	0.822	0.784	0.765	0.747	0.730	0.713	0.697	0.681	0.665	0.650	0.635	0.621	0.593	0.567	0.543	0.519	0.497	0.476	0.437	0.402	0.328	0.269
6	0.888	0.837	0.790	0.746	0.725	0.705	0.685	0.666	0.648	0.630	0.613	0.596	0.580	0.564	0.535	0.507	0.480	0.456	0.432	0.410	0.370	0.335	0.262	0.207
7	0.871	0.813	0.760	0.711	0.687	0.665	0.644	0.623	0.603	0.583	0.565	0.547	0.530	0.513	0.482	0.452	0.425	0.400	0.376	0.354	0.314	0.279	0.210	0.159
8	0.853	0.789	0.731	0.677	0.652	0.627	0.604	0.582	0.561	0.540	0.521	0.502	0.484	0.467	0.434	0.404	0.376	0.351	0.327	0.305	0.266	0.233	0.168	0.123
9	0.837	0.766	0.703	0.645	0.618	0.592	0.567	0.544	0.522	0.500	0.480	0.460	0.442	0.424	0.391	0.361	0.333	0.308	0.284	0.263	0.225	0.194	0.134	0.094
10	0.820	0.744	0.676	0.614	0.585	0.558	0.533	0.508	0.485	0.463	0.442	0.422	0.404	0.386	0.352	0.322	0.295	0.270	0.247	0.227	0.191	0.162	0.107	0.073
11	0.804	0.722	0.650	0.585	0.555	0.527	0.500	0.475	0.451	0.429	0.408	0.388	0.369	0.350	0.317	0.287	0.261	0.237	0.215	0.195	0.162	0.135	0.086	0.056
12	0.788	0.701	0.625	0.557	0.526	0.497	0.470	0.444	0.420	0.397	0.376	0.356	0.337	0.319	0.286	0.257	0.231	0.208	0.187	0.168	0.137	0.112	0.069	0.043
13	0.773	0.681	0.601	0.530	0.499	0.469	0.441	0.415	0.391	0.368	0.346	0.326	0.307	0.290	0.258	0.229	0.204	0.182	0.163	0.145	0.116	0.093	0.055	0.033
14	0.758	0.661	0.577	0.505	0.473	0.442	0.414	0.388	0.363	0.340	0.319	0.299	0.281	0.263	0.232	0.205	0.181	0160	0.141	0.125	0.099	0.078	0.044	0.025
15	0.743	0.642	0.555	0.481	0.448	0.417	0.389	0.362	0.338	0.315	0.294	0.275	0.256	0.239	0.209	0.183	0.160	0.140	0.123	0.108	0.084	0.065	0.035	0.020
16	0.728	0.623	0.534	0.458	0.425	0.394	0.365	0.339	0.314	0.292	0.271	0.252	0.234	0.218	0.188	0.163	0.141	0.123	0.107	0.093	0.071	0.054	0.028	0.015
17	0.714	0.605	0.513	0.436	0.402	0.371	0.343	0.317	0.292	0.270	0.250	0.231	0.214	0.198	0.170	0.146	0.125	0.108	0.093	0.080	0.060	0.045	0.023	0.012
18	0.700	0.587	0.494	0.416	0.381	0.350	0.322	0.296	0.272	0.250	0.230	0.212	0.195	0.180	0.153	0.130	0.111	0.095	0.081	0.069	0.051	0.038	0.018	0.009
19	0.686	0.570	0.475	0.396	0.362	0.331	0.302	0.277	0.253	0.232	0.212	0.194	0.178	0.164	0.138	0.116	0.098	0.083	0.070	0.060	0.043	0.031	0.014	0.007
20	0.673	0.554	0.456	0.377	0.343	0.312	0.284	0.258	0.235	0.215	0.196	0.178	0.163	0.149	0.124	0.104	0.087	0.073	0.061	0.051	0.037	0.026	0.012	0.005

where: NPV = net present value
B = benefits for year 0
B_1, B_2, B_n = benefits for years 1, 2, ..., n
C = costs for year 0
C_1, C_2, C_n = costs for years 1, 2, ..., n

11.

$$\text{B:C Ratio} = \frac{\left(\frac{B_1}{(1+r)} + \frac{B_2}{(1+r)^2} + \cdots \frac{B_n}{(1+r)^n}\right)}{\left(\frac{C_1}{(1+r)} + \frac{C_2}{(1+r)^2} + \cdots \frac{C_n}{(1+r)^n}\right)}$$

12. Avrom Bendavid-Val, Regional and Local Economic Analysis for Practitioners, New and Expanded Edition (New York: Praeger, 1983), p. 153.

13. J. Price Gittinger, Economic Analysis of Agricultural Projects, EDI Series in Economic Development, published for the Economic Development Institute of the World Bank (Baltimore and London: John Hopkins Press, 1982), p. 3-4.

14.

$$\text{IRR} = B - C + \frac{B_1-C_1}{(1+r)} + \frac{B_2-C_2}{(1+r)^2} + \cdots \frac{B_n-C_n}{(1+r)^n} = 0$$

15. Gittinger, Economic Analysis of Agricultural Projects, p. 332.

16. Under certain circumstances, it is possible that more than one discount rate will make the present values equal zero. This has been one of the criticisms of the IRR technique.

17. Gittinger, Economic Analysis of Agricultural Projects, p. 336 (words in parentheses added).

18. Interpolation can also be done geometrically, as shown below.

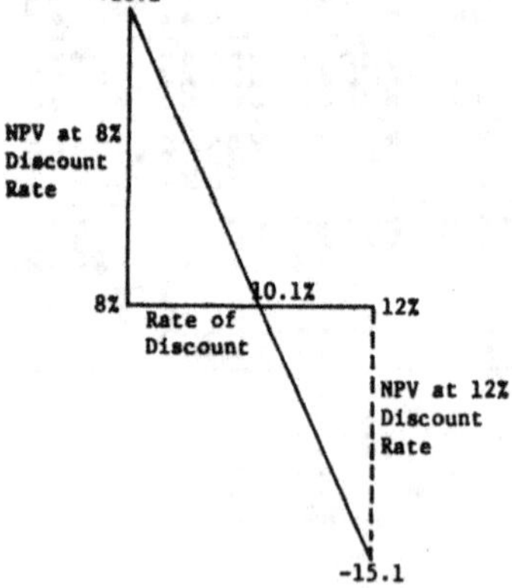

The x axis shows the range of the discount rates, beginning with the lower discount rate. The y axis gives the net present values of the lower and higher discount rates. The net present values for the lower discount rate are positive, and for the higher discount rates they are negative. The point where the higher and the lower NPVs intersect on the x axis provides the discount rate at which the net present values would equal zero.

19. Michael P. Todaro, Economic Development in the Third World (London: Longman Group Limited, 1977), p. 155. Todaro defines opportunity cost in the following words:

> in production, the real value of resources used in the most desirable alternative--e.g., the "opportunity cost" of producing an extra unit of manufactured good is the output of, say, food that must be foregone as a result of transferring resources from agricultural to manufacturing activities; in consumption, the amount of one commodity that must be foregone in order to consume more of another.

20. Bendavid-Val, Regional and Local Economic Analysis, p. 155.

21. Projects in this category have often been referred to as "soft" projects. Noting the difficulties in appraising them, Olof Marelius writes in An Institutional Approach to Project Analysis in Developing Countries (Paris: OECD, 1981), p. 58:

> This trend [emphasis on soft sectors] affects pre-investment work in several ways. Surveys, prefeasibility studies and project preparation have become considerably more complex, and data are hard to get. . . . The Bank [World] has traditionally been equipped to finance projects in hard infrastructure, where the contours and limits of the project itself have been sharper and relevant institution-building simpler. Work in education and rural development is considerably more complex and necessitates a broader coverage.

22. Thomas R. Leinbach and Robert C. Cromley, "A Goal Programming Approach to Public Investment Decisions: A Case Study of Rural Roads in Indonesia," Socio-Economic Planning Sciences, An International Journal, Vol. 17, No. 1, 1983, pp. 1-10.

23. The article points out that the Indonesian Rural Works projects are aimed at injecting cash wages into very

poor areas, and enlarging development opportunities for the local residents. Recently more importance has been attached to the overall development impact that will accrue as a result of the construction of infrastructure projects. See Leinbach and Cromley, ibid., p. 3.

24. In the basic model, the weighting factor for each variable is set equal to one. Subsequent versions of the basic model relax these assumptions by utilizing the weighting capability. See Leinbach and Cromley, ibid., p. 6.

25. The basic model is solved as a mixed-integer programming problem. According to the authors, the main feature of the goal programming approach is its flexibility and generality. See Leinbach and Cromley, ibid., pp. 6 and 16.

26. Mark S. Thompson, Benefit-Cost Analysis for Program Evaluation (Beverly Hills: Sage Publications, Inc., 1980), p. 225.

27. Ministry of Local Government and Rural Development, Special Public Works Programme; Criteria and Conditions for Project Identification, Circular no. 5, Government of Bangladesh, Dacca (undated draft under discussion).

CASE EXERCISE: PAVING THE GRAVEL ROAD

The Planning Officer of Gotonia District has proposed to the District Council a project for paving a small strip of road, about 2 km, that connects two relatively important towns in his district. At present, it is a gravel road. Details of the project's costs and benefits are given below.

Question 1. Read the project details and do the following exercises:

1. The details as presented are haphazard and somewhat nonsequential. Reorganize them on the basis of the outline given in Chapter 2, or in any other way that would enable the District Council to understand what the project is all about, and decide whether or not to accord its approval to the project.
2. Calculate the project's net present value and benefit-cost ratio at a 15 percent rate of discount. Use the Discounting Table given on page 113 of this chapter and the blank forms attached to this exercise.
3. Taking note of the economic situation in your country, would you recommend using a rate of discount higher than 15 percent? Give reasons.
4. Find the internal rate of return.
5. Under "Project Benefits," it is stated that the benefits of the project consist primarily of (a) reduced vehicle operating costs and (b) the avoidance of the maintenance costs of the gravel road. What other benefits are likely to accrue from this project?
6. Suggest criteria for evaluating this project, if you think the benefit-cost approach is inappropriate (see page 109).

DETAILS OF THE PROJECT

Proposed Project and Costs

The towns are presently connected by a 2 km gravel road. The gravel road is in reasonably good condition, although in summer dust forces the vehicles to keep a substantial distance between them. The width of the road is 3 m; it has several grades of about 8-10 percent and a few sharp curves. Traffic in 1982 averaged about 70 vehicles per day. Trucks and buses can travel at an average speed of 25 km/hr, and passenger cars at 30 km/hr. There is no railway alternative.

It is now proposed to pave the entire 2 km road, and make certain improvements in the alignment. If the project is approved, work on paving the road will begin in year 10 and be completed by the end of the year. The cost of paving the road is estimated at TK500,000/km.

The maintenance costs of the paved road are estimated at TK12,500/km annually, or TK25,000 for the entire 2 km road. Every five years, that is, in years 15, 20, and 25, the road will be paved almost anew, the economic cost of which is estimated at TK150,000. The life of the project is 20 years. There is no salvage value thereafter.

Traffic

Taking into account the past growth trends in traffic, it is estimated that truck and bus traffic on the new paved road will increase by 12 percent annually from year 9 to the first five years of the project, at 10 percent annually in the second five years of the project, and 8 percent during the remaining years of the project. For passenger cars, increases of 15, 12, and 9 percent are expected for these respective periods of the project.

In addition, some additional traffic is likely to be generated by the expansion of economic activities in the area. During the first three years of the project, the generated traffic is likely to be about 10, 15, and 20 percent of the normal traffic, and after the third year, the generated traffic would be 20 percent per year. Estimates of the new generated traffic are shown in Table 1. Also shown in the table are figures of normal traffic for selected years.

Project Benefits

The benefits of the project consist <u>primarily</u> of (a) reduced vehicle operating costs, and (b) the avoidance of the maintenance costs of the gravel road.

<u>Reduced Vehicle Operating Costs</u>. Table 2 presents data on the operating costs of various kinds of vehicles.

The unit benefits for the normal traffic are thus about

TABLE 1
Estimates of traffic, 1982-2003

Year	Project Year	Trucks		Buses		Cars		Total
		Normal	Generated	Normal	Generated	Normal	Generated	
9	-	45	-	10	-	15	-	70
10	0	50	-	11	-	17	-	78
11	1	56	6	12	1	20	2	97
12	2	63	10	13	2	23	4	115
13	3	71	14	15	3	27	5	135
16	6	99	20	21	4	40	8	192
21	11	157	31	34	7	69	14	312
30	20	316	63	68	14	149	30	640

TABLE 2
Vehicle operating costs (in TK/km)

Type of Road	Trucks	Buses	Passenger Cars
Paved	1.58	1.99	0.89
Gravel 1982	2.48	3.09	1.19

TABLE 3
Benefits as a result of the reduced vehicle operating costs (in TK/km)

Years	Trucks	Buses	Passenger Cars
Upto 16	0.90	1.10	0.30
After 16*	1.12	1.36	0.38
After 21*	1.46	1.76	0.50

*Vehicle-operating costs on the gravel road would increase after 1989 and again after year 21 on account of increased congestion. Benefits, therefore, should be estimated higher than the start of the project.

TK0.90/km for trucks, TK1.10/km for buses, and TK0.30/km for cars. The benefits are likely to increase after year 16 of increased operational costs on the gravel road. These are shown in Table 3. For generated traffic, the unit benefits are assumed to be one-half of the above.

The total benefits from reduced vehicle operating costs for the first year of the project are shown below:

Normal Traffic

56 trucks	x 2 km	x 365 days	x TK0.90	=	TK36,800
12 buses	x 2 km	x 365 days	x TK1.10	=	TK 9,600
20 cars	x 2 km	x 365 days	x TK0.30	=	TK 4,400
			Subtotal	=	TK50,800

Generated Traffic

6 trucks	x 2 km	x 365 days	x TK0.45	=	TK 2,000
1 bus	x 2 km	x 365 days	x TK0.55	=	TK 400
2 cars	x 2 km	x 265 days	x TK0.15	=	TK 200
			Subtotal	=	TK 2,600
			Grand Total	=	TK53,400

Maintenance Costs of the Gravel Road. Maintenance expenditures of the gravel road are increasing and would increase rather sharply as traffic grows. Taking into account all related factors, it is estimated that annual maintenance costs would increase from TK12,000/km in year 11 to TK20,000/km in year 16, and TK24,000/km in year 21 to TK27,000/km in year 30.

Other benefits from the project such as time saved on each trip because of the better road have been recognized but not explicitly considered in evaluating this project.

Question 2. Calculate the project's net present value and benefit-cost ratio at a 15 percent rate of discount.

Step 1. Estimate the traffic by types of vehicles.

Year	Trucks		Buses		Cars	
	Normal	Generated	Normal	Generated	Normal	Generated
--						
10						
11						
12						
13						
14						
15						
16						
17						
18						
19						
20						
21						
22						
23						
24						
25						
26						
27						
28						
29						
30						

Note: Source of data Table 1.

Step 2. Calculate costs and benefits

Year	Costs (TK,000)			Benefits (TK,000)		
	Capital	Maintenance	Total	Reduced Operating Costs	Avoided Maintenance Costs	Total
9						
10						
11						
12						
13						
14						
15						
16						
17						
18						
19						
20						
21						
22						
23						
24						
25						
26						
27						
28						
29						
30						

Notes: For costs: See Section 1.

For benefits: See Section 3.

{Per km vehicle operating cost x 365 x traffic }
{Per km avoided maintenance cost x 365 x traffic}

Step 3. Find out the discounted values of 1 at a 15 percent rate of discount (see the relevant column on the Discounting Table, page 113).

Step 4. Multiply the total costs and total benefits with the relevant discounted values.

Year	Total Costs	Total Benefits	Discounted Values of 1 at 15% Rate of Discount	Present Values		Net Present Value
				Total Costs	Total Benefits	
9						
10						
11						
12						
13						
14						
15						
16						
17						
18						
19						
20						
21						
22						
23						
24						
25						
26						
27						
28						
29						
30						

Step 5. Find out the benefit-cost ratio.

Results: Net present value at
15 percent rate of discount =

Benefit-cost ratio (with a
15 percent rate of discount) =

Question 3. Determine the internal rate of return.

Year	Total Costs	Total Benefits	Discounted Values at	
			Higher Rate of Discount	Lower Rate of Discount
9				
10				
11				
12				
13				
14				
15				
16				
17				
18				
19				
20				
21				
22				
23				
24				
25				
26				
27				
28				
29				
30				

Note: Use formula given on page 98.

Solution to Question 2

Step 1. Estimates of traffic by types of vehicles

Year	Trucks		Buses		Cars	
	Normal	Generated	Normal	Generated	Normal	Generated
9	45		10		15	
10	50		11		17	
11	56	6	12	1	20	2
12	63	10	13	2	23	4
13	71	14	15	3	27	5
14	80	16	17	3	31	6
15	90	18	19	4	36	7
16	99	20	21	4	40	8
17	109	22	23	5	45	9
18	120	24	25	5	50	10
19	132	26	28	6	56	11
20	145	29	31	6	63	13
21	157	31	34	7	69	14
22	170	34	37	7	75	15
23	184	37	40	8	82	16
24	199	40	43	9	89	18
25	215	43	46	9	97	19
26	232	46	50	10	106	21
27	251	50	54	11	116	23
28	271	54	58	12	126	25
29	293	59	63	13	137	27
30	316	63	68	14	149	30

Step 2. Estimates of costs and benefits

(Unit: TK1,000)

Year	Project Year	Costs			Benefits		
		Capital	Maintenance	Total	Reduced Vehicle Operating Costs	Avoided Maintenance Costs	Total
9	-						
10	0	1,000	-	1,000	--		
11	1		25	25	53	24	77
12	2		25	25	61	27	88
13	3		25	25	71	30	101
14	4		25	25	80	34	114
15	5		150	150	91	37	128
16	6		25	25	100	40	140
17	7		25	25	137	42	179
18	8		25	25	150	43	193
19	9		25	25	166	45	211
20	10		150	150	184	46	230
21	11		25	25	199	48	247
22	12		25	25	281	49	330
23	13		25	25	305	49	354
24	14		25	25	330	50	380
25	15		150	150	356	51	407
26	16		25	25	376	51	427
27	17		25	25	417	52	469
28	18		25	25	450	53	503
29	19		25	25	488	53	541
30	20		25	25	527	54	581

Step 3. Discounted values of 1 (see column 5)

Step 4. Discounted costs and benefits (see columns 6 and 7)

Year	Project Year	Total Costs	Total Benefits	Discounted Values of 1	Discounted Present Values		Net Present Value
					Costs	Benefits	
9	-						
10	0	1,000		1.00	1,000		-1,000
11	1	25	77	.870	21.8	67.0	45.2
12	2	25	88	.756	18.9	66.5	47.6
13	3	25	101	.658	16.5	66.5	50.0
14	4	25	114	.572	14.3	65.2	50.9
15	5	150	128	.497	74.6	63.6	-11.0
16	6	25	140	.432	10.8	60.5	49.7
17	7	25	179	.376	9.4	67.3	57.9
18	8	25	193	.327	8.2	63.1	54.9
19	9	25	211	.284	7.1	59.9	52.8
20	10	150	230	.247	37.0	56.8	19.8
21	11	25	247	.215	5.4	53.1	47.7
22	12	25	330	.187	4.7	61.7	57.0
23	13	25	354	.163	4.1	57.7	53.6
24	14	25	380	.141	3.5	53.6	50.1
25	15	150	407	.123	18.5	50.1	31.6
26	16	25	427	.107	2.7	45.7	43.0
27	17	25	469	.093	2.3	43.6	41.3
28	18	25	503	.081	2.0	40.7	38.7
29	19	25	541	.070	1.8	37.9	36.1
30	20	25	581	.061	1.5	35.4	33.9
					1,265.1	1,115.9	-149.2
1	2	3	4	5	6	7	8

Step 5.

Net present value = discounted benefits-discounted costs
= TK1,115,900 - TK1,265,100
= -TK149,200

Benefit-cost ratio = discounted benefits/discounted costs
= TK1,115,900/TK1,265,100
= 0.882

Solution to Question 3

Step 1. Estimates of discounted values at two discount rates

Year	Discounted Values at			
	Higher Rate of Discount 15%		Lower Rate of Discount 5%	
	Costs	Benefits	Costs	Benefits
9	1,000	--	1,000	
10	21.8	67.0	23.8	73.3
11	18.9	66.5	22.7	79.8
12	16.5	66.5	21.6	87.3
13	14.3	65.2	20.6	93.8
14	74.6	63.6	117.6	100.4
15	10.8	60.5	18.7	104.4
16	9.4	67.3	17.8	127.3
17	8.2	63.1	16.9	130.7
18	7.1	59.9	16.1	136.1
19	37.0	56.8	92.1	141.2
20	5.4	53.1	14.6	144.5
21	4.7	61.7	13.9	183.8
22	4.1	57.7	13.3	187.6
23	3.5	53.6	12.6	191.9
24	18.5	50.1	72.2	195.8
25	2.7	45.7	11.5	195.6
26	2.3	43.6	10.9	204.5
27	2.0	40.7	10.4	209.3
28	1.8	37.9	9.9	214.3
29	1.5	35.4	9.4	219.0
	1,265.1	1,115.9	1,535.7	3,020.6

Step 2.

$$IRR = \text{Lower Rate of Discount} + \left(\begin{array}{c}\text{Difference Between}\\ \text{the Discount Rates}\end{array}\right)\left(\frac{\begin{array}{c}\text{Net Present Value at}\\ \text{the Lower Discount Rate}\end{array}}{\begin{array}{c}\text{Sum of Net Present Values}\\ \text{at the Two Discount Rates}\end{array}}\right)$$

$$= 5 + (10)\,\frac{1,484,900}{1,484,900 + 149,200}$$

$$= 5 + (10)\,(.9086)$$

$$= 5 + 9.086$$

$$= 14.086$$

4
Who Benefits from Projects?

THE NEW CONCERNS IN PROJECT ANALYSIS

Consider the case of a minor irrigation project that has been found to be profitable in financial as well as economic terms. According to the calculations made by project analysts, the project is expected to yield an internal rate of return of 12 percent, a rate that is considerably higher than the prevailing interest rate in the domestic market. The project is capable of recouping its capital in less than five years. Its benefit-cost ratio works out to be greater than one, and so on. The question is whether planners, on the basis of this information, are in a position to accept this project and recommend it to the local banks for sanction of a loan. Is this information on profitability adequate for planners to make a decision on the project?

Or, take another example of two projects that have varying rates of return. Should the project having a higher internal rate of return be invariably preferred to the other one? Or, are there other aspects of the project that planners need to look at?

Until around the beginning of the Second Development Decade, such questions, if raised, would have posed little or no problems for planners and practitioners. The guiding principle for project selection was profit maximization. All that the planners had to do was to rank the competing projects, in ascending or descending order, according to the rates of return, and to draw cut-off lines on the basis of the availability of resources. In principle, such rules were ordinarily not expected to be tampered with.

Since the 1970s, however, the entire field of project planning has undergone extraordinary changes, and the kinds of questions referred to in the above have, as a result, gained enormous significance. The principle of profit maximization is no longer the sole criterion for the selection of local development projects. A set of new concerns have sprung up on the scene. What has happened in the intervening years to change the situation? Why has the need for additional criteria for project selection arisen? It is important for local level planners and administrators to come to grips with this changed situation, and then to consider what these criteria are and how they should be applied for purposes of evaluating and selecting local level development projects.

A brief historical background to the changes that have recently occurred in the discipline of project planning would thus be useful at the very outset of this chapter. As mentioned above, until the beginning of the Second Development Decade, the dominant criterion for project selection, the one that was widely employed in several developing countries, was the capacity of the project to earn or generate a surplus that was the difference between the expected value of its output and input. The higher the capacity, the better the project was considered. This criterion evolved out of the principal objective of development, which, in most developing countries, was to increase the aggregate per capita incomes of the people. Increase in per capita incomes was considered synonymous with increased welfare. The criterion fitted in well with the emphasis of countries on "growth" and "growth-related" objectives. Also, the medium-term plans of the countries did not pay much attention to the distributive aspects of growth in determining development objectives, nor was any attempt made to incorporate such aspects in project selection criteria. Problems related to income disparities, spatial inequalities, and skewed distribution of basic services were not of special importance to the countries. Galal A. Amin, a well-known development economist, describes this situation by giving a quote from Jan Tinbergen[1] made twenty-four years ago:

> The general principle to be followed should be to maximize the contribution of the investment programme to the country's well-being. Well-being may be taken to mean national income, present and future, with possible corrections for its distribution over social groups or regions. Since these corrections will have to be incidental in most cases, not much can be said about them in a general way. . . . Leaving this for what it is, we will concentrate on the <u>aim of a maximum</u>

national product or incomé, present and future. [Emphasis added]

Following Tinbergen and many other economists of that time, attention was directed in the countries to make the "cake larger," and to many, to use Amin's words again, "it seemed almost wasted effort to discuss how to divide a cake which was too small in the first place."

By the early 1970s, there was worldwide dissatisfaction with income growth as a measure of, or even as a means to, improved welfare. It manifested itself in two ways. First, the concept of income as a measure of welfare or development came to be seriously questioned. Development planners who had been observing the pattern of growth in developing countries recognized the fallacy of equating "income growth" with "development," and argued that the concept of development was much broader, and embraced many facets in addition to income. Second, it became increasingly clear that whatever growth had taken place in developing countries was distributed in an equitable manner. Advocates of growth had assumed that its fruits would trickle down to the poorest but this assumption had proven to be erroneous. Growth did not trickle down. People at the lowest rung did not improve their levels of living. Income distribution showed little improvement, and, in fact, worsened in some countries.[2] Scholars explained this phenomenon by noting that although there was not necessarily a conflict between growth and development, it was clear that rapid growth itself did not bring about more equitable distribution. "Trickle-down, if it existed was a long time coming."[3]

The net result of this planning experience over a period of 15-20 years was a broader, although not unanimous, agreement among planners and policymakers to introduce and incorporate distributive aspects in their countries' planning systems. The question they faced was whether they could do so via changes in the macrolevel policies and strategies. One argument was that the distributive aspects legitimately belonged to the field of macroeconomics, and, therefore, if these have to be introduced, macroeconomic policies should be appropriately changed, modified, and strengthened. For instance, if planners considered income distribution in a specific country skewed in favor of the rich, what they had to do was to change fiscal policies and the country's tax structure in ways designed to eliminate skewness. Or, if certain parts of the country were poor and underdeveloped, the remedy lay in changing the fiscal and financial policies in favor of such areas.

The argument opposed to this view was that the developing countries, assuming that they were serious about distributive aspects, would not be able to change macroscopic policies in favor of the "poor," "disadvantaged," and the "bypassed" groups and areas, because they are "soft" and not in a position to take hard decisions that are implicit in such an approach. Their institutional framework is weak. Also, forces opposed to such changes are very strong, and, if pressed, could pose threats to the government. According to the proponents of this argument, although it was not easy to change macroeconomic policies, distributive aspects could be introduced by making changes in the project (microlevel) planning techniques. Since then this view has been sustained, encouraging planners to broaden, refine, and strengthen the project selection criteria and techniques.

Support to the broadening of the project selection criteria has also been lent on somewhat different considerations. David Potts, otherwise a serious critic of this view,[4] justifies broadening of the project selection criteria on the grounds that the alternative to this is a strategy that would place no premium on distribution. He says that

> the use of social analysis,[5] even if somewhat arbitrary and undemocratic, is likely to give results that are more beneficial to the mass of the population, despite rather than because of government objectives. The second and perhaps more important justification is that any adequately conducted social analysis should provide valuable information about the distribution effects of development projects, which, if freely available, can be helpful in indicating either the sort of projects to be encouraged, or avoided, or the reforms which such projects make necessary.[6]

The status of project analysis has thus undergone a change resulting from the experiences and developments in the developing countries. There now exists a view that the expanded scope of project analysis can serve as a substitute for macroeconomic actions; what is not so clear is whether the expanded scope has come to stay or represent merely a transitional phase in the planning systems of the developing countries.

THE EXPANDED SCOPE OF PROJECT ANALYSIS: ITS THESIS AND COMPONENTS

That the scope of project analysis stands today vastly expanded is evident from the brief historical review given above. The principal theme of the present thinking on the subject is that projects should be evaluated with respect to the manner in which they may affect people and areas belonging to different economic and social status. Merely ascertaining their financial and economic profitability is not adequate. The latter may be adequate in countries that are marked by no appreciable differences in the levels of economic and social development, or whose populations are largely homogeneous. But it is inadequate for countries that are characterized by inequalities and disparities of various sorts. For such countries, project selection criteria need to be expanded.

"Who will benefit most from the project" lies at the center of the expanded scope of project analysis. Will the benefits of the project accrue largely to the high-income population group or the low-income population group, or both? In what proportions would the various groups benefit? Will the project benefit the landless and marginal farmers or the farmers who already have three, or four hectares of land? Will the benefits of the project extend to the relatively poorer or the richer parts of the District, Upa-Zilla, or the Municipio? Such concerns constitute the thrust of the present thinking on project analysis.

If we analyze these concerns in an operational framework, we would find that it is possible to conveniently group them in three sets of criteria. These are:

<u>Capacity of the Project to Generate Higher Incomes for the "Poor"</u>: The underlying purpose of this criterion is obviously to use it in order to select projects that would favor the poorer sections of the concerned local area. The greater the capacity of the project to generate incomes for the poor, the better would be the project. This criterion is linked with the overall goal of reduction in poverty and income disparities.

<u>Capacity of the Project to Benefit the "Less-Developed"[7] Sections of the Local Area</u>: This criterion draws its

justification from the goals concerning balanced spatial development. As in the above, the objective in using this criterion is to assign higher weights to projects that are expected to benefit the relatively less developed parts of the area and accelerate the process of their development.

Capacity of the Project to Create Local Employment: The intent of including this criterion in project selection is to use it to select projects that have a greater potential for creating local employment. Creation of local employment has, of late, become an important objective of development in a number of countries, and is being used as a surrogate for objectives such as "incomes for the poor," "people's participation in development," and "human dignity."

By no means do these three sets of criteria capture the highly complex scene in the developing countries. There are other criteria, too, that in many ways are just as important as those mentioned above. For instance, the capacity of projects to use local and indigenous resources is an extremely important objective in several countries. Projects selected on the basis of this criterion serve the general objectives of self-reliance, reduction of external dependence, and savings on scarce foreign exchange. In many countries, involvement of the people in development is being talked about as an end in itself. If projects are to be selected to serve this objective, then a different set of criteria will need to be formulated. For reasons of space, time, as well as the view that consideration of so many criteria would unduly complicate the task of local-level planners and strain their resources, this volume focuses on the methodology of using the above-mentioned three sets of criteria.

HOW TO USE THE DISTRIBUTION CRITERIA? THE WEIGHTING SYSTEM

It is interesting to point out that although there is a broader acceptance in the countries of the view that the distributive aspects of a project are important, and should form an integral part of project analysis, there is virtually no agreement on how this should be done. The past few years have seen a number of international agencies, particularly the World Bank, the United Nations Industrial Development Organization, and the International Fund for Agricultural Development, as well as several individual scholars, devote their attention on developing methodologies for incorporating such aspects within the scope of project analysis. However, their efforts have produced little of operational value. Their main contribution has been to suggest a kind of "weighting system" wherein a higher weight could be assigned to projects that are likely to benefit the "poor," and, conversely, a lower weight to projects whose benefits are likely to accrue to the "rich." Where only one project is under consideration, its benefits, according to the system, should be weighted along the same lines, that is, by assigning a higher weight to that part of the benefits that, in the estimates of the project analysts, may accrue to the poorer sections and a lower weight to the richer sections of the local community. The basis for decision should be the sum of the weighted benefits thus arrived at. According to the scholars, this is one way in which the distributive aspects of projects can be brought within the scope of analysis; in this sense, the weighting system becomes a device to initially classify projects' outputs and benefits according to the various categories of beneficiaries, and subsequently to revalue them on the basis of the "weights."

What the weighting system implies is that planners, if they wish to use it for evaluating projects for their distributional effects, should:

1. find out the project's aggregate unweighted benefits
2. estimate the expected share of each category of beneficiary (rich or poor; landless, marginal farmers, or large farmers; etc.) in the aggregate unweighted benefits
3. determine weights for each category of beneficiary
4. calculate the weighted benefits for each category of beneficiary, by multiplying the estimated share of the beneficiary by its corresponding weight
5. Add the weighted benefits for each category of beneficiary to arrive at the project's aggregate weighted benefits
6. use the project's aggregate weighted benefits for purposes of decision making

Let us take the example of two projects to illustrate the above-mentioned steps (Example 6). In a simplified form, the application of the weighting system would involve such estimates and calculations. Thus, in Example 6, Proj-

Example 6. The Weighting System

Steps	Project A			Project B		
1. Find out the unweighted aggregate benefits (TK,000)	TK2,200			TK3,000		
2. Estimate the share of each category of beneficiary in unweighted aggregate benefits	Categories of Beneficiaries					
	High income farmers	Medium income farmers	Low income farmers	High income farmers	Medium income farmers	Low income farmers
	250	450	1,500	1,400	800	800
3. Determine weights	1	2	3	1	2	3
4. Calculate weighted benefits for each category of beneficiary	250	900	4,500	1,400	1,600	2,400
5. Aggregate weighted benefits	TK5,650			TK5,400		

ect A would appear to be a better choice if weighting is applied; in the absence of any weighting of the benefits, Project B would appear to be a preferable option.

Although the weighting system carries a common man's logic, it encounters in practice serious problems and difficulties of definition, data, and methodology. Alluding to the problems in using the weighting system, Galal Amin points out that:[8]

> To identify all gainers and losers as well as their income groups in any but a very rough way, and to allocate to each group its share in the total, will prove a very difficult if not an impossible task. Every project has a host of primary, secondary and tertiary beneficiaries and losers, with each benefit and cost having its own multiplier effect. This identification and allocation has to be done for every year of the project's life, since both beneficiaries and

> losers may change from year to year as well as their income groups. The weights themselves may have to be changed with the changes in income distribution caused by the project itself or by other factors.

In Amin's view:

> The biggest problem is of course to decide what weights to apply. The choice of distribution weights cannot obviously be regarded as an objective judgement of fact. . . . If the distribution weights are to be at all meaningful they have to be taken to convey subjective judgements of the relative importance of one person's consumption compared with another's. The problem then becomes one of deciding whose subjective judgement to take.

After examining its various pros and cons, Amin considers a weighting system "utterly unnecessary," and explains it with the following example:

> Let us, for instance, attach any weights we like to the benefits accruing to the poor from having access to better housing facilities as compared with those accruing to higher income groups from building a luxury hotel in town. Whatever relative weights we may use, if they result in admitting building the hotel and rejecting the provision of better housing for the poor, we may not be satisfied. We will suspect that our weights must have been "wrong" and we may go on changing them until we want the result we want. In other words, distribution weights can never have an independent information value but are (if meaningful) simply one way to expressing a relative evaluation of two specific alternatives.
>
> Amin reminds us of Voltaire's ironical remark that
>
> witchcraft can be used to kill a herd of sheep provided they are given some arsenic at the same time. Similarly, you can choose among projects by using distribution weights provided you have made up your mind already which project is the more desirable.[9]

WHO BENEFITS FROM PROJECTS? THE BASIC MINIMUM STEPS

If the "weighting system" is fraught with so many problems and difficulties, then what should planners do to evaluate projects from the distributional standpoint? How should they proceed in the matter?

Before discussing the basic minimum steps implicit in using the "who benefits from projects" criteria, two points should be made to begin with. First, the need for this kind of an evaluation arises only when the benefits of any project under consideration are expected to accrue to not only the "poor" but other sections of the local community as well. The need for this kind of evaluation will not arise in cases where projects have been prepared and designed especially or exclusively for the "poor," as seems to be the trend in many developing countries. For such projects, a cost-effective approach would be adequate. Second, to be able to undertake an evaluation of projects from the standpoint of distribution would inevitably require data on (1) the structure of population according to income levels or any other basis planners may consider relevant for identifying the "poor," and (2) the share of the project's benefits likely to accrue to the "poor" in relation to the other sections of the local community. Without data on these two components, projects cannot be evaluated from this standpoint. So, if in a particular situation, planners find it impossible to gain access to this kind of data or even make rough estimates, it would be advisable to abandon consideration of projects from the distributional viewpoint.

In the earlier part of this chapter, three sets of criteria were referred to that reflected the concern of local planners for distributive or equity considerations in project selection. These were (1) capacity of the project to generate higher incomes for the "poor," (2) capacity of the project to benefit the "less-developed" sections of the local area, and (3) capacity of the project to create local employment. Let us examine how we can use these criteria, specifically in relation to the following:

1. The steps involved in using them
2. The requirements of data for each of the steps
3. The methods for processing of data, and their complication for use by planners and decision makers

CAPACITY OF THE PROJECT TO GENERATE HIGH INCOMES FOR THE "POOR"

The raison d'etre for this criterion is well established. The fruits of economic development have been shared unequally by different sections of the local community. The local-level planners have now to evaluate every project proposal to ascertain (1) whether or not it would benefit the poorer sections, and (2) in what proportion it would benefit them in comparison to the "rich."

Four steps are involved in evaluating projects from this standpoint:

Step 1. Establish norms for the identification of the "poor."

Step 2. Categorize local population according to the established norms.

Step 3. Find out the aggregate outputs and services of the concerned project(s).

Step 4. Estimate the share of project's outputs and services likely to accrue to each category of population.

Setting up of norms for identifying the "poor" (Step 1), and categorization of population on the basis of those norms (Step 2) constitute the initial task in evaluating projects from the distributional viewpoint. It is a task that is indispensable; at the same time, it is not possible to suggest or lay down any universal norms for identifying the "poor," as the situation differs widely from country to country. Poverty norms are normally specific to the country in question. For instance, some countries define poverty levels in terms of per capita incomes, and in others poverty is expressed in terms of people's accessibility to certain basic facilities and services. In some situations, planners have attempted to use "calorie intake" and "life expectancy" for determining the levels of poverty.

In a paper written for the United Nations, Food and Agricultural Organization (FAO), John McArthur has come up with six different ways for measuring poverty. Due to their relevance at the local level, four are briefly mentioned next.

A Threshold Minimum Level of Per Capita Disposable Income. This measure indicates that level of income that is considered necessary to allow individuals to obtain a sufficient supply of those consumption and household investment items that are normally purchased from private income, and which are necessary to support a given minimum level of personal consumption.

A Minimum Level of Per Capita Consumption. This measure, which is a direct alternative to per capita income levels, lays down minimum levels of per capita consumption, and allows for the fact that these levels may be more or less than the value of aggregate per capita income.

Definition Based on the Notion of Basic Needs. The Declaration of Principles and Programmes of Action adopted by the 1976 World Employment Conference at Geneva specified items of basic needs, which may provide a clue to defining poverty. According to the Declaration, these include: (1) certain minimum requirements for private consumption such as food, shelter, and clothing; and (2) essential services provided by and for the community including safe drinking water, sanitation, public transport, public health, and educational and cultural facilities. According to MacArthur, this approach is, in a sense, more comprehensive, as it recognizes that there are certain basic needs that must be met if the population is not to be categorized as "poor."

Definition based on Social, Ethnic, or Occupational Status. This measure defines poverty groups according to the social, ethnic, or occupational status of the population. In many countries, there are special tribes and castes who are considered poor on account of their status. In others, certain occupational groups are considered disadvantaged. United Nations Children's Fund (UNICEF) has in the past few years started a program for the upliftment and involvement of women in the development process on the ground that they, as a social group, have not benefited from development. In the context of Bangladesh, the Dutch Ministry of Foreign Affairs laid down that "for all practical purposes a sufficiently useful indication of poverty is arrived at by concentrating on the amount of land a family owns. . . . Two and a half acres have been taken as the point to draw the line, and all families owning less than 2.5 acres, or no land at all, fall below the poverty line."

For each of these methods, it is possible to construct simple formats such as the ones shown in Format 11. Hard statistics on these aspects may not be available, but it is adequate to make rough estimates of the number of people below the poverty line, or in different categories according to their status, or the levels of services and facilities accessible to them.

Many additional formats are possible. What is important to recognize is that there are many ways in which the "poor," the "disadvantaged," and the "bypassed" groups can be identified. It depends on the purpose of identification, as well as the context of the project. If planners are evaluating, for instance, an irrigation project, the relevant format to use would be Format 11-D.

Two points should be noted with respect to these steps. First, in most, if not all, cases, norms for identifying the "poor" (often called the target groups) are laid down at national levels; the local level planners and functionaries rarely have the flexibility to use their own norms for this purpose. They are expected to follow the established norms, and make estimates of the numbers of the "poor" and to analyze data on their status, characteristics, etc. Second, the classification of population on the lines suggested in these formats does not require collection of any new sets of data and information. It is based on data collected during the household and village level surveys to which a reference was made in Chapter 2 of this volume. Household and village surveys, although carried out for purposes of generating project ideas, contain a wealth of information on aspects such as income, occupation, social status, and accessibility to services. The same sets of data can be utilized for categorizing the population of the local areas.

Once the norms for identifying the "poor" have been established, and population categorized according to those norms, the next task (steps 3 and 4) is to find out the expected outputs and services of the project, and to allocate them to the different categories of population. This is the most difficult and yet crucial stage in project analysis. There are no rules or formulae for these steps. Estimates have to be made on the total volume of outputs and services expected from the project (a consolidated figure for the duration of the project or for the individual years), and these have to be allocated to the different population categories.

Take the case of an irrigation project, which, let us assume, will produce x cusec of water/day. In order to evaluate this project from the distributional standpoint, planners will need to make estimates on the relative shares of x cusec of water for (1) the landless, (2) the marginal and small farmers, and (3) the large farmers, that is, the proportion in which x cusec of water may be utilized by the various categories of farmers--such as shown in Figure 13.

Format 11. Identification of the "Poor"

A. According to Income Categories

Income Categories	Classification of Population According to Income Categories	
	Number	Per cent
High-income (> than .... income)		
Average-income (Range ..... income)		
Low-income (< than .... income)		
Total		100.0

B. According to Nutrition

Nutrition Levels	Classification of Population According to Nutrition Levels	
	Number	Per Cent
Above-average (> than .... income)		
Average (Range ..... income)		
Below-average (< than .... income)		
Total		100.0

C. According to "Access to Social Services and Facilities" Categories.

Items of Social Services and Facilities	Classification of Population According to the Access to Social Services			
	Number		Per Cent	
	Acces-sible	Inacces-sible	Acces-sible	Inacces-sible
Potable water supply				
Primary school (within ... minutes of walking distance from the place of residence)				
Health centre (within ... minutes of walking distance from the place of residence)				
....				

D. According to Social Status (Land/Animal Holdings)

Status Categories	Classification of Households According to Social Status (Land/Animal Holdings)	
	Number	Per Cent of Total Farmer/ Households Under Study
LAND		
Large-holding farmer households (>than .. hectares)		
Average-holding farmer households (Range ... hectares)		
Small-holding farmer households (<than .. hectares)		
Landless tenant households		
Total		
ANIMALS		
Affluent households (>than .. animal heads)		
Average households (Range ... animal heads)		
Poor households (<than .. animal households)		
Households without any animal heads		
Total		

E. According to Occupations, Castes, Ethnicity, and Sex

Examples of the 'Poor' According to Occupations, Castes, Ethnicity and Sex	Classification of Population According to the Occupations, Castes, Ethnicity and Sex	
	Number	Per Cent of Total Population
Scavengers (occupation)		
Scheduled castes in some countries (ethnicity)		
Specific tribes in some countries (ethnicity)		
Women (considered bypassed and disadvantaged according to several UN agencies)		

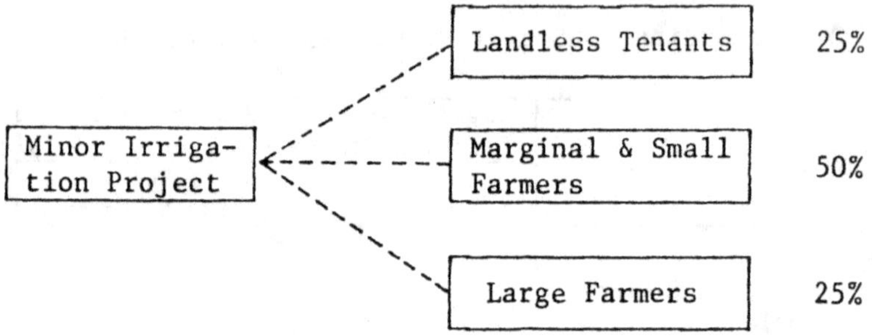

Figure 13. Accrual of benefits

Estimates of the above type are critical to distributional analysis. This step amounts to making the best possible judgment on who the beneficiaries of the project might be. The objective is not to aim at precision, which is neither necessary nor possible, but to make the best possible estimate on the accrual of benefits to the different categories of population.

As for the other types, formats can be used for this step as well. Sample prototypes are given in Formats 12 and 13.

Data from these steps set the stage for planners to make decisions on the candidate projects. Is the share of the "poor" in the project's outputs and benefits adequate? Do planners consider the income-generating capacity of the concerned project for the relatively poorer sections large enough for its inclusion in the list of accepted projects? Planners can even juxtapose the existing situation with the future expected situation, and determine whether or not the project will serve the distributional objectives.

Examine Example 7. Several points can be noted from this table.

1. The project, if accepted, would benefit all groups of farm households. In aggregate, therefore, the project would appear sound.
2. The large farm households will reap a greater share of benefits in comparison with the other two groups. Their incomes will increase by 120 percent as compared to 116 percent in the incomes of small and average farmer households and 115 percent in the incomes of the landless tenant households.
3. Income distribution in the area will worsen. The share of landless tenant households in the average incomes will decline from 69.9 percent to 68.6

Format 12. Estimated Share of Various Categories of Beneficiaries in Project's Net Discounted Benefits

Categories of Beneficiaries	Net Discounted Benefits (TK,000)	
	(TK,000)	Per Cent to Total
High-income (>than ... income)		
Average-income (Range .... income)		
Low-income (< than ... income)		
Total		100.0

Format 13. Allocation of Project's Output to Different Categories of Beneficiaries (Irrigation Project)

Categories of Beneficiaries	Project's Output (x Cusec of Water)	
	Cusec of Water	Per Cent to Total
Large-holding farmer households (>than ... hectares)		
Average-holding farmer households (Range .... hectares)		
Small-holding farmer households (< than ... hectares)		
Landless tenant households		
Total		100.0

percent, while it will remain more or less the same for the small and average farmers and increase for the large farm households.

These facts will constitute the basis for decision making by planners and administrators. When there are several project proposals needing decisions, it will be necessary for planners to bring together the data for all projects, and compare which projects serve the "poor" most, and which projects contribute most to the objectives of local development (Format 14).

Example 7. Assessing Possible Effects of an Irrigation Project on Various Categories of Beneficiaries

Categories of Beneficiaries	Current Level of Income		Additional Income Per Household Expected to be Generated as a Result of the Project	Projected Level of Income	
	Income Per Household ($)	As a Proportion of the Average Income Per Household		Income Per Household ($)	As a Proportion of the Average Income Per Household
Large-holding farmer households (30 in number)	$200	139.9%	$40	$240	143.3%
Small- and average-holding farmer households (60 in number)	$150	104.9%	$25	$175	104.5%
Landless tenant farmer households (50 in number)	$100	69.9%	$15	$115	68.6%
Average per household	$143		$24.6	$167.5	

Format 14. Arrangement of Projects According to the "Who Benefits" Criterion

Candidate Projects	Net Discounted Benefits*	Categories of Beneficiaries*		
		High-Income	Average-Income	Low-Income
A B C D E F				

* These classifications can be adapted according to the types of projects under consideration.

Capacity of the Projects to Benefit the "Least-Developed" Sections of the Concerned Local Area

Planners often express their concern for equity or distribution criterion in terms of space rather then income. Concern for spatial equity criterion has gained considerable importance, possibly due to the fact that disparities in the levels of living among various parts of the developing countries have widened enormously over the years, and created social and political tensions of various sorts. As a result, serious attempts are being made in the developing countries to redress such widening spatial disparities by assigning preference to projects that are likely to benefit the relatively less developed parts of the local areas and communities.

Evaluation of projects from the standpoint of spatial equity criterion involves five steps:

Step 1. Establish indicators for the identification of the less-developed, poor, and backward parts of the concerned local area (District, Upa-Zilla, or Tambon).

Step 2. Delineate the concerned local area according to the established indicators.

Step 3. Find out the aggregate project's outputs and services.

Step 4. Allocate the project's outputs and services to different categories of areas.

There are extensive explanations in the literature on the subject as to what indicators should be used for delineation of areas according to the levels of development (Step 1), and how to use those indicators (Step 2). Some authors have suggested the use of single indicators such as "income" for purposes of delineation, particularly in situations where the single indicator can faithfully represent the levels of development of the constituent parts of the area, region, or the country. Others have pointed out the need for using multiple indicators because of the inability of a single indicator to truly capture the development levels of the constituent parts.

At local levels, income data for smaller spatial units of the concerned local areas are unlikely to be available; also, the relevance of income data for local levels is questionable. More relevant at these levels would be data on the availability of economic and social infrastructure; the relative backwardness of the area can be determined on the basis of the availability and adequacy of the various infrastructure and other services and facilities (Format 15).

Format 15. Identification of the "Less-Developed" Parts of the Concerned Local Area

A. According to the Availability and Adequacy of Economic Infrastructure*

Items of Economic Infrastructure	Parts of the Local Area (Sub-Divisions)		
	I	II	III
1. Length of primary roads/ 1,000 population			
2. Per cent of villages not connected by primary road			
3. Per cent of villages not connected by power connections			
4. Area covered by irrigation as per cent of total area under irrigation			
5. Number of agriculture extension and service centre centres/1,000 population			

* The line of distinction between economic and social infrastructure is thin.

B. According to the Availability and Adequacy of Social Infrastructure*

Items of Social Infrastructure	Parts of the Local Area (Sub-Divisions)		
	I	II	III
1. Number of primary schools/ 1,000 population			
2. Per cent of villages without a primary school (within ... minutes of walking distance)			
3. Number of health centres/ 1,000 population			
4. Per cent of villages without a health centre (within ... minutes of walking distance)			
5. Per cent of villages without drinking water supply sources (within ... minutes of walking distance)			

* The line of distinction between economic and social infrastructure is thin.

Many more indicators can be added, where necessary. On the other hand, if there are one or two indicators that sum up the general level of socioeconomic development, then it would be adequate to use them at local levels. Data on these aspects are also available in the village surveys to which reference has been made in Chapter 2. It is largely a question of looking through the village survey sheets and pulling out the relevant data.

From here on, the analysis runs along the same lines as shown for the income distribution criterion. If it is proposed that the project is to be located in one of the relatively less developed parts, then such an evaluation may be considered unnecessary. However, if the projects' benefits are likely to be shared by the district as a whole, then a judgment on which sections would benefit most will be necessary. Again, where several projects are under consideration, data for all of them can be arranged to determine which projects will benefit the least developed parts of the most, and appropriate decisions can be made. An indicative format is given in Format 16. With this set of data, it would be possible for planners to make a judgment as to which project serves the objective of balanced spatial development the best.

Format 16. Arrangement of Projects According to the Criterion of Spatial Distribution of Project's Outputs or Services

Candidate Projects	Total Projects Outputs or Services	Project's Outputs or Services to to Accrue to:		
		Most-Developed Part	Average-Developed Part	Least-Developed Part
A				
B				
C				
D				
E				
F				

Capacity to Create Local Employment

This criterion under the generic caption of "Who Benefits from Projects"[11] requires a somewhat different type of data and analysis. The purpose of introducing this criterion is to determine the project's capacity to create local employment, the implication being that projects that have a higher capacity to create local employment should be preferred over others.

It should be pointed out that this criterion, in itself, will not show the strengths or weaknesses of the project unless it can be interpreted in relation to either the project's outputs and services or investments. The strengths or weaknesses of a project can be assessed by finding out the number of local jobs per unit of output and services, or per unit of investment that it is expected to generate (Format 17). The use of this criterion will require a three-step analysis.

Step 1. Estimate the "local employment" likely to be generated by the project in question.

Step 2. Find out the project's (a) expected outputs or services, and (b) expected investments.

Format 17. Arrangement of Projects According to Their Capacities to Generate Local Employment

Candidate Projects	Expected Local Employment		Wages as a Per Cent of Total Input Costs
	Per Unit of Capital Investment	Per Unit of Project's Outputs or Services	
A			
B			
C			
D			
E			
F			

Step 3. Divide "local employment" by project's (a) expected outputs or services, and (b) expected investments.

It is through this kind of analysis that projects can be evaluated from the distributional standpoint. Two concluding observations should now be made. First, there is a significantly high elements of estimates and judgment here. As mentioned in the preface to this volume, at every stage in project analysis and planning planners have to make estimates and judgment. These are inevitable in all planning exercises. Whether it is the question of finding out how much a project would cost and what benefits would it produce, or of determining the stream of costs and benefits over the expected lifespan of the project, or who the beneficiaries of the project might be--at every stage, estimates are essential. No less important is the role of "judgment": Is a 12 percent return adequate? Should a project that increases the incomes of the "poor" by only 5 percent be accepted? And so on. The analysis is, therefore, inevitably speculative but essential.

Second, excepting those cases when planners may formulate projects exclusively or specifically for the "poor" or the less-developed areas, there is no escape from making estimates on who the project's beneficiaries might be. Even a rough assessment on the distributional aspects is better then no assessment at all. Its advantages have already been pointed out earlier in this chapter. It helps in selecting the right kinds of projects. It assists in redesigning the projects if the analysis shows that they may not benefit the "poor."

NOTES

1. Galal A. Amin, "Project Appraisal and Income Distribution," World Development, 1978, Vol. 6, No. 2, Cost-Benefit Analysis and Income Distribution in Developing Countries: A Symposium, Edited by J. D. MacArthur and Galal A. Amin.

2. Income distribution data of selected countries are given below.

Country	Year	Percentage Share of Household Income, by Decile Groups of Households										Gini coefficient
		1st (lowest)	2nd	3rd	4th	5th	6th	7th	8th	9th	10th (highest)	
Argentina	1970	1.5	2.9	4.3	5.4	6.3	7.8	10.3	11.2	15.1	35.2	0.44
Bangladesh	1973-74	2.7	4.1	5.1	6.3	7.6	8.5	10.2	13.3	14.8	27.4	0.35
Brazil	1972	0.6	1.4	2.1	2.9	4.0	5.4	7.1	9.9	16.0	50.6	0.61
Fiji	1977	1.1	2.6	4.0	4.8	6.0	7.4	9.4	11.5	15.5	37.8	0.47
India	1975-76	2.5	3.4	4.5	5.8	6.4	7.5	9.0	11.5	15.8	33.6	0.42
Kenya	1976	0.9	1.8	2.6	3.7	4.9	6.6	8.9	10.3	14.6	45.8	0.59
Republic of Korea	1976	1.8	3.9	5.0	6.2	7.1	8.3	9.9	12.5	17.8	27.5	0.38
Mexico	1968	0.7	2.0	2.8	3.6	4.5	5.7	7.5	10.6	15.9	46.7	0.56
Nepal	1976-77	1.8	2.8	3.4	4.6	5.2	6.5	7.5	9.0	12.7	46.5	0.53
Philippines	1970-71	1.9	3.2	4.1	4.9	5.8	7.0	8.5	10.5	15.3	38.8	0.46
Sri Lanka	1969-70	3.1	4.4	5.4	6.3	7.3	8.4	9.8	11.9	15.1	28.3	0.35
Zambia	1976	1.0	2.4	2.9	4.5	5.2	6.0	7.6	9.3	14.8	46.3	0.56

Source: International Labour Office, World Employment Report 1, 1984, Geneva.

3. See Mike Veitch, "Cost-Benefit Analysis and Basic Needs," p. 19, IDS Bulletin, August 1978, Vol. 10, No. 1, Special Issue by the Project Planning Centre, University of Bradford.

4. David Potts, "Politics, Social Cost-Benefit Analysis and Planners," in IDS Bulletin, August 1978, Vol. 10, No. 1, Special Issue by the Project Planning Centre, University of Bradford.

5. According to David Potts, "Social analysis is concerned with the distribution of income between savings and consumption, and between different income groups," ibid.

6. Ibid.

7. The terms "poor" and "less-developed" are used here in the generic sense.

8. Galal A. Amin, "Project Appraisal and Income Distribution."

9. Ibid.

10. John D. MacArthur, "Who are the rural poor, how shall we recognize them, and who needs to know anyway," Discussion Paper, No. 29, Project Planning Centre for Developing Countries, University of Bradford, October 1978.

11. "Who benefits from projects" has more generally been referred to as "Social analysis" in literature. Social analysis is concerned with the distribution of income between saving and consumption, and between different income groups. According to Colin Bruce ("The Stages of Project Planning: An Introduction to Project Planning," Economic Development Institute Training Materials, The International Bank for Reconstruction and Development, Washington, D.C., 1980, p. 23-24),

> the financial and economic analyses both tacitly assume that a dollar or a rupee or a baht has the same social value for a poor person as a rich person. They also assume that a dollar used for private consumption has the same value as a dollar saved and as a dollar in the hands of the government. What social cost-benefit does is to remove one or more of these assumptions. . . . What social analysis does is to attach a greater weight to benefits:
>
> - which go to poor people rather than rich people
> - which are saved rather than spent immediately on consumption goods.

EXERCISE 1

In the recently prepared Draft Plan, the District Council of Gotonia has stressed the need for environmental protection and conservation. Through the Planning Officer, the Council has directed district-level functionaries to screen all project proposals from the standpoint of environmental protection and conservation, implying that projects that are likely to damage the environment should be either rejected or given low priority.

The district-level functionaries, not being able to visualize how this directive should be taken into account in project selection, have sought the assistance of a planning officer, and want him to do the following:

1. Operationalize this directive into specific sets or subsets of criteria.
2. Indicate what exactly this new objective of "environmental protection and conservation" would bring to the District of Gotonia.
3. Identify steps for evaluating candidate projects from the standpoint of environmental protection and conservation.
4. Develop formats for compilation and analysis of information.

You are the planning officer for purposes of this exercise.

EXERCISE 2

In his book, Regional and Local Economic Analysis for Practitioners, Avrom Bendavid-Val has provided an example of a Project Evaluation Framework. The example relates to projects for improving local marketplaces in rural areas.

Parts of the framework are reproduced below. Examine the framework with specific reference to the questions listed here:

1. Can this framework be effectively used at local levels in your country?
2. If yes: identify data requirements for each indicator given in the framework.
3. If no: (a) state reasons, and (b) redesign the framework that you think could be used in your country.

Example of a Project Evaluation Framework

Potential Projects to Improve Local Marketplaces in Rural Areas: Project Evaluation Framework	
I. Eligibility Criteria	Indicators
A. Is the marketplace of an eligible type?	.Marketplace must serve predominantly the local area, not wholesaling for export from the region
B. Is the marketplace in a currently eligible location?	.Marketplace must be in a town of 5,000 people or less
C. Is the project within current financial limits?	.Project must cost ... or less
II. Preference Criteria	Indicators
A. Cost-effectiveness	.What are the project's benefit-cost ratio and internal rate of return: financial, economic, socioeconomic?
B. Promotion of growing prosperity	.When will the project be self-sustaining? .Are the necessary skills available for the long-term management of the project? .Will the project continue to be needed and provide benefits over many years?
C. Equity	.How many and what proportion of the beneficiaries of the project each year are estimated to be poor people?
D. Private sector stimulation	.How much private sector investment will be stimulated by the project in its first five years?
E. Employment	.How many new permanent jobs will be created: direct, indirect, induced?
F. Regional integration	.How will the project benefit other regional sectors? .How will the project benefit other subareas of the region? .Will the project strengthen a regional node? .How will the project strengthen the overall economy of the region?
G. Participation	.Place an X in the boxes of the matrix below to indicate phases of the project in which participation of groups at different levels is technically possible.

		Project phases		
		Generation of project ideas (pre-feasibility)	Identification	Preparation
Level of participation	Beneficiary groups			
	Local leadership			
	Local government			
	Private sector			
	Regional government			
	National government			
	Others			

Source: Adapted from Avrom Bendavid-Val, Regional and Local Economic Analysis for Practitioners, New and Expanded Edition (New York: Praeger, 1983), pp. 144-5.

5
The Checklist Approach: Final Step Toward Decision Making

THE CHECKLIST APPROACH

What information should be collected by local level planners in their search for development projects, and how that information should be processed and analyzed constituted the hub of discussions in the earlier chapters. We discussed in this regard a cross-section of methods and approaches, providing illustrations, examples, and formats of how use could be made of them. These discussions have brought us, therefore, to a stage at which we should have, for every project proposal, a folder (usually a file) consisting of wide-ranging data on the financial, economic, social, locational, and other important aspects. If compiled on the lines indicated, the folder should have information on the project's profitability. It should contain information on the propensity of the project to benefit the "poor." There should also be data on the project's capacity to generate local employment. References to the type of resources the project would make use of should also be available in the folder. And so on.

Note should be taken of the fact that information in the folder is voluminous. It has been collected and processed not by one single or composite team of planners and project analysts, but by several teams of functionaries who are specialists of sorts, having knowledge and understanding of the sectors to which they belong. Until this stage in project analysis, no attempt has been made by anyone at the local level to put together, aggregate or synthesize this information. It is unwieldy and, to a large extent, fragmented.

A stage, however, arrives in project analysis and planning when all this unwieldy and fragmented information has to be put together and synthesized. Without this stage, planners, administrators, and decision makers can do little with the folder in terms of decision making. No decision maker, whether he is the Planning and Development Officer, or the Agricultural Officer for an Upa-Zilla in Bangladesh, has the necessary time and resources to examine the vast quantities of information, coalesce and consolidate the same, and then make a decision on the project. The decision maker needs to have an executive summary, a kind of digest of key data on every project proposal for purposes of decision making. He needs to view the proposal not in part, but in totality. For him, identification and consolidation of key data are indispensable stages in project analysis.

A question arises as to how local level planners should identify the key data from the mass of information that the folder contains, and later organize it in a way that it may provide the decision makers with a total view of the project in question. The total view does not imply compilation of every bit of information that has been collected at various stages of project analysis. Nor does it mean preparation of a summary of the project's folder. It is highly selective, and consists of only those data that help decision making. It is decision oriented.

One of the ways in which it may be possible to construct a total view of a project is through what is called here a "checklist approach." The purpose underlying the checklist approach is to provide decision makers with key data on every proposal, thus enabling them to make a decision on the project's suitability to the local area. As the title of the approach suggests, it involved first a prudent selection of indicators that, in the view of planners, are decision oriented, and second, pulling out of the folder information on each of the indicators. The checklist has to be prepared in such a way that:

1. It is comprehensible.
2. It is comparable with the checklists of other candidate projects.
3. It facilitates decision making.

How do we select the list of indicators? What parts of the analysis provide information on them? How should that information be organized?

SELECTION OF INDICATORS FOR THE CHECKLIST

It should be underlined once again that the selection of indicators for the checklist is an extremely important step in making decisions on the candidate projects. Any faulty selection of indicators, or an attempt on the part of the planners to either over- or underplay any specific aspect would result in wrong choices of projects. It is therefore important for planners to give serious attention to the process of selection of indicators. Having stated this, it is equally necessary to point out that the question of the selection of indicators is not something that arises only at this stage of project analysis; rather, it runs through all stages beginning with project identification. For instance, reference was made in Chapter 2 to a series of criteria for screening projects. Chapter 3 discussed profitability measure as a criterion for evaluating projects. Similarly, in the preceding chapter, a number of criteria relating to the distributive aspects of projects were brought up for discussion. These criteria are nothing else but indicators, out of which a few, the key ones, have to be chosen for inclusion in the checklist. The indicators, in a sense, represent what planners want to accomplish through projects. The selection of indicators is, therefore, not a new task for planners.

Mention should also be made of the fact that the checklist approach does not warrant collection of any new set of information. It relies wholly on information that planners have collected and analyzed during various stages of project analysis, and which forms a part of the project's folder. This approach does not point to gaps in data; rather, it utilizes the existing data for decision making.

Indicators can be grouped broadly into several categories according to their characteristics. Thus, it becomes possible to use the categories shown on the next page.

These categories, together with the indicators shown against them, are merely suggestive. Depending on the development priorities and strategies for the area, the number of categories or the indicators or both can be increased, decreased, or modified. There is neither any rigidity nor universality about them. These reflect the planners' perception of the role of projects in local development, and, therefore, these are necessarily area and situation specific.

CATEGORIES	INDICATORS
I. FINANCIAL AND ECONOMIC VIABILITY AND COST-EFFECTIVENESS	Payback period Internal rate of return (a) Financial (b) Economic Net present value per unit of total investment Index of goal-achievement per unit cost
II. IMPACT ON BENEFICIARIES	Principal beneficiary Share of various categories of beneficiaries in project's output (a) Low-income families (b) Average-income families (c) High-income families Relative increase in incomes of various categories of beneficiaries as a result of the project (a) Low-income families (b) Average-income families (c) High-income families
III. LOCAL EMPLOYMENT GENERATION	Local employment intensity Wages as a per cent of total input costs
IV. LOCAL RESOURCE UTILIZATION	Local resource intensity Costs of local raw materials as a per cent of total input costs
V. SPATIAL IMPACT	Location Extent to which the project will benefit the less-developed parts of the local area
VI. LINKAGES	Linkages with other projects
VII. GESTATION PERIOD	Period within which the project would become operational

FOUR WAYS TO READ THE CHECKLIST FOR DECISION MAKING

Once the indicators have been identified, the next task is obviously to examine the project's folder for data on each of them. Sources of data on each indicator are known; one needs to simply extract them from the folder and place them against the indicator. It is here that the question arises as to how the data are to be used, and in what way the decision makers should read the information on the checklist. Examine in this connection the checklist of a hypothetical integrated rural development project given in Example 8.

The data given in Example 8 are of an integrated rural development project. The project's capital investments are estimated at $600,000. Its main activities include the provision of infrastructure, agriculture support facilities and services, community health programs and facilities, and family planning. The question is: How do we analyze the following checklist of Example 8? What decision can be reached on the basis of the data given in the example on this project?

There are at least five alternative ways in which we can read and analyze the checklist in Example 8.

Consider the Data in the Checklist in Toto

One of the most effective ways for planners is to consider the data given in the checklist as a whole, and take a view as to whether or not the project should be accepted. The strength of this method lies in the fact that it allows planners to look at the totality of the project. That is,

1. What would it produce? (nature of the project's output)
2. How much would it produce? (financial and economic viability)
3. At what cost would it produce? (new present values per unit of total investment)
4. For whom would it produce? (impact on beneficiaries)
5. Where would it produce? (spatial impact)

Example 8. Checklist of a Hypothetical Integrated Rural Development Project

I. FINANCIAL AND ECONOMIC VIABILITY AND COST-EFFECTIVENESS	
Payback period	30 months
Internal rate of return	
(a) Financial	10.8 per cent
(b) Economic	17.8 per cent
Net present value per unit of total investment	...
Index of goal-achievement per unit cost	...
II. IMPACT ON BENEFICIARIES	
Principal beneficiary	Low-income farm families 5,000 out of 8,500 families
Share of various categories of beneficiaries in project's output	
(a) Low-income families	54.0 per cent
(b) Average-income families	38.8 per cent
(c) High-income families	7.2 per cent
Relative increase in incomes of various categories of beneficiaries as a result of the project	
(a) Low-income families	11.5 per cent
(b) Average-income families	11.0 per cent
(c) High-income families	8.0 per cent
III. LOCAL EMPLOYMENT GENERATION	
Local employment intensity	High
Wages as a per cent of total input costs	28 per cent
IV. LOCAL RESOURCE UTILIZATION	
Local resource intensity	High
Costs of local raw materials as a per cent of total input costs	28 per cent
V. SPATIAL IMPACT	
Location	Underdeveloped area
Extent to which the project will benefit the less-developed part of the local area	...
VI. LINKAGES	
Linkages with other projects	High
VII. GESTATION PERIOD	
Period within which the project is expected to become operational	12 months

6. By what strategy would it produce? (local resource utilization and local employment intensity)
7. How soon would it produce? (gestation period)

These are the critical variables for decision making. The weakness of this method is that it does not permit easy comparability between projects.

Compare the Data in the Checklist with Present Norms or Standards Laid Down by Planners for Project Selection

In some countries, planners and administrators often prescribe norms for project selection. Under this method, the checklists of the candidate projects can be juxtaposed against the prescribed norms, and projects that satisfy the norms can be recommended for selection (see Format 18). This method is weak insofar as it introduces a rigidity in the project selection procedures. Local situations may require norms to be modified that generally may not be possible under this method. Also, prescribing norms may itself be arbitrary.

Compare Checklists of all Candidate Projects, and Select the Most Promising Ones

In order to select the most promising projects, planners may compare the checklists of all candidate projects by rearranging data in the manner shown in Format 19. Even though a comparison between projects is inevitable in any method that may be employed for selection of projects, application of this method presents several problems. For instance, a project may appear promising on indicators 1-5, but not so promising on 6-13. A second project may show poor performance on indicators 1-5, but good performance on indicators 6-13. A third one may present a different picture. Comparisons of such situations are hardly possible by this method.

Provide Numerical Ranks or Values to Every Indicator, and Consolidate the Values for Purposes of Decision Making

According to this method, data on the checklist can be assigned numerical values (1, 2, 3, ...), and aggregated to arrive at one single value or number, which can then serve as the basis for decision making.

Format 18. Comparison of Project's Data with Preset Norms

	Project A	Norms
I. FINANCIAL AND ECONOMIC VIABILITY AND COST-EFFECTIVENESS		
Payback period		
Internal rate of return		
(a) Financial		
(b) Economic		
Net present value per unit of total investment		
Index of goal-achievement per unit cost		
II. IMPACT ON BENEFICIARIES		
Principal beneficiary		
Share of various categories of beneficiaries in project's output		
(a) Low-income families		
(b) Average-income families		
(c) High-income families		
Relative increase in incomes of various categories of beneficiaries as a result of the project		
(a) Low-income families		
(b) Average-income families		
(c) High-income families		
III. LOCAL EMPLOYMENT GENERATION		
Local employment intensity		
Wages as a per cent of total input costs		
IV. LOCAL RESOURCE UTILIZATION		
Local resource intensity		
Costs of local raw materials as a per cent of total input costs		
V. SPATIAL IMPACT		
Location		
Extent to which the project will benefit the less-developed part of the local area		
VI. LINKAGES		
Linkages with other projects		
VII. GESTATION PERIOD		
Period within which the project is expected to become operational		

Format 19. Comparing Checklists of Candidate Projects

	Project A	Project B	Project C
I. FINANCIAL AND ECONOMIC VIABILITY AND COST-EFFECTIVENESS			
Payback period Internal rate of return (a) Financial (b) Economic Net present value per unit of total investment Index of goal-achievement per unit cost			
II. IMPACT ON BENEFICIARIES			
Principal beneficiary Share of various categories of beneficiaries in project's output (a) Low-income families (b) Average-income families (c) High-income families Relative increase in incomes of various categories of beneficiaries as a result of the project (a) Low-income families (b) Average-income families (c) High-income families			
III. LOCAL EMPLOYMENT GENERATION			
Local employment intensity Wages as a per cent of total input costs			
IV. LOCAL RESOURCE UTILIZATION			
Local resource intensity Costs of local raw materials as a per cent of total input costs			
V. SPATIAL IMPACT			
Location Extent to which the project will benefit the less-developed part of the local area			
VI. LINKAGES			
Linkages with other projects			
VII. GESTATION PERIOD			
Period within which the project is expected to become operational			

The hypothetical checklist given earlier can be used to illustrate this method. In the example provided, the project showed an internal rate of return of 10.1 percent. Planners can put a value on this figure (1, 2, or 3), depending on whether they consider this to be low, medium, or high. For instance, planners may like to use scales such as the following:

High:	Medium:	Low:
More than 20%	10-20%	Less than 20%
Value: 3	Value: 2	Value: 1

According to this scale, the 10.1 percent IRR would receive a value of 2. Other indicators can likewise be assigned numerical values as shown in Appendix 5-B.

Application of the numerical values to the data of the hypothetical integrated rural development project gives it a score of 41 out of a total of 44, as may be seen in Table 15. This score can then serve as the basis for decision making as well as for comparison with other candidate projects. The limitation of this method is that it relies almost entirely on numbers and quantities, which are not always the most appropriate for making decisions on projects. Also, it may not be possible to assign numbers to some of the indicators, the net present value as a percent of total investment being one of them.

What method should be employed for consolidation of key data is a decision that needs to be made at local levels, and by those who are responsible for local development. Every method has its strong as well as weak points. What is important for planners to recognize is the need for project evaluation from varying standpoints, taking a total, rather than partial, view on the candidate projects.

TABLE 15
Summary of scores attained (corresponding to the checklist of the hypothetical integrated rural development project)

Category	Score Attained	Maximum Score
I. Financial and economic viability	7	9
II. Impact on beneficiaries	14	15
III. Local employment effects	6	6
IV. Local resource utilization	6	6
V. Spatial impact	3	3
VI. Linkages	2	2
VII. Gestation period	3	3
Total	41	44

Appendix 5-A. Executive Summary for . . . . . Project

Proposed by: . . . . . . Department

I. GENERAL

TITLE . . . .

SECTOR . . . .   SUBSECTOR . . . .

IMMEDIATE OBJECTIVE

INITIAL CAPITAL INVESTMENT . . . .

AVERAGE ANNUAL OPERATING INVESTMENT . . . .

NATURE OF THE PROJECT'S OUTPUT/SERVICE . . . .

GESTATION PERIOD . . . .

II. FINANCIAL AND ECONOMIC VIABILITY AND COST-EFFECTIVENESS

PAY-BACK PERIOD (1)*. . . . .   (2)**. . . . .

INTERNAL RATE OF RETURN (1)*. . . . . .   (2)**. . . . .

COST-EFFECTIVENESS IN RELATION TO ALTERNATIVE MEANS OF ACHIEVING THE SAME OBJECTIVE   HIGH | MEDIUM | LOW

III. IMPACT ON BENEFICIARIES

PRINCIPAL BENEFICIARY . . . .

SHARES OF VARIOUS CATEGORIES OF BENEFICIARIES IN PROJECT'S OUTPUTS/SERVICES   [ ] [ ] [ ]

IV. LOCAL EMPLOYMENT GENERATION

LOCAL EMPLOYMENT INTENSITY	HIGH / MEDIUM / LOW
WAGES AS A PER CENT OF TOTAL INPUT COSTS	

V. LOCAL RESOURCE UTILIZATION

LOCAL RESOURCE INTENSITY	HIGH / MEDIUM / LOW
COSTS OF LOCAL RAWMATERIALS AS A PER CENT OF TOTAL INPUT COSTS	

VI. SPATIAL IMPACT

LOCATION . . . .
EXTENT TO WHICH THE PROJECT WILL BENEFIT THE LESS-DEVELOPED PART OF THE LOCAL AREA . . . .

VII. SECTORAL AND INTERSECTORAL LINKAGES

LINKAGES WITH OTHER PROJECTS	HIGH *	LOW **	NIL ***

II * Financial ** Economic

VII * Complementary ** Competitive *** Substitute

Appendix 5-B. Table of Scores

Category/Indicator	Score
I. FINANCIAL AND ECONOMIC VIABILITY AND COST-EFFECTIVENESS	
Payback Period (3)	
36 months and less	3
36-60 months	2
60 months and more	1
Internal Rate of Return (6) (financial and economic)	
20 per cent and more	3
10-20 per cent	2
10 per cent and less	1
Cost-Effectiveness (3)	
High	3
Average	2
Low	1
II. IMPACT ON BENEFICIARIES	
Principal Beneficiaries (3)	
Low-income families	3
Average-income families	2
High-income families	1
Share of the various categories of beneficiaries in project's output (6)	
50 per cent and more	3
25-50 per cent	2
25 per cent and less	1
Relative change in incomes of the various categories of beneficiaries as a result of the project (6)	
20 per cent and more	3
10-20 per cent	2
10 per cent and less	1
III. LOCAL EMPLOYMENT EFFECTS	
Local employment intensity (3)	
High	3
Average	2
Low	1
Wages as a per cent of total input costs (3)	
20 per cent and more	3
10-20 per cent	2
10 per cent and less	1

Categories/Indicator	Score
IV. LOCAL RESOURCE UTILIZATION	
Local resource intensity (3)	
High	3
Average	2
Low	1
Cost of local rawmaterials as a per cent of total input costs (3)	
20 per cent and more	3
10-20 per cent	2
10 per cent and less	1
V. SPATIAL IMPACT	
Location (3)	
Less-developed part	3
Average	2
More-developed part	1
Extent to which the project will benefit the less-developed part of the local area (3)	
50 per cent and more	3
25-50 per cent	2
25 per cent and less	1
VI. LINKAGES	
Linkages with other projects (3)	
High	2
Low	1
Nil	0
VII. GESTATION PERIOD	
Period within which the project is expected to become operational (3)	
12 months and less	3
12-24 months	2
24 months and more	1

CASE EXERCISE: INTEGRATED RURAL DEVELOPMENT PROJECT FOR GOTONIA DISTRICT (IRDPGD) IN THE REPUBLIC OF GOTONIA

The Chairman of the District Council of Gotonia desired to see the "folder" on the IRDPGD. Notwithstanding the various explanations of the Planning Officer of Gotonia District that the folder consisted of loose sheets of notes, tables, and rough computations, and that the folder may not be comprehensible, the Chairman insisted on seeing the folder "as it was."

As contended by the Planning Officer, the folder turned out to be disorganized. Some aspects of the IRDPGD had been explained with write-ups, while others were presented in the form of tables, statements, and rough calculations. When the Chairman could not obtain a clear picture on the project from the folder, he asked the Planning Officer to prepare for him and members of the Council an Executive Summary.

Attached here are a "few sheets" on the project. Based on the information contained in the attached sheets, you should do the following:

1. Prepare an Executive Summary on the Integrated Rural Development Project for Gotonia District.
2. Give your recommendations on the project together with the underlying justification.

Note: All calculations should be carefully rechecked. Sheets containing the calculations should be provided with the Executive Summary. Use the format of the Executive Summary given in Appendix 5-A.

Integrated Rural Development Project for Gotonia District in the Republic of Gotonia

Introduction to the Proposal

A countrywide review of the past development efforts and strategies that the Republic of Gotonia undertook last year showed that most development efforts were characterized by "isolated projects" and "actions," and that the various sectoral programs implemented in the different parts of the country were prepared with little or no linkages/connections with other sectors or projects. The Republic felt that this situation should be remedied by establishing integrated development programs; accordingly it decided to set up its first broad-based integrated rural development project in Gotonia District.

In pursuance of this decision, the Government of the Republic of Gotonia invited a mission from the Interregional Bank who, together with a team from the Gotonia Civil Service, drew up the project, which was called the "Integrated Rural Development Project for Gotonia District (IRDPGD)." The project area was chosen in a way that it coincided with the boundaries of the administrative region of the District of Gotonia. In designing the project, the team took into account the agricultural practices prevalent in the region and drew upon the results of research on production technologies carried out under similar conditions elsewhere in the country.

Subject to its acceptance, the IRDPGD will most likely receive assistance from the Interregional Bank and its former colonial ruler to supplement its own local resources. A number of state-owned financing institutions and commercial banks are also expected to extend financial support to the project.

Country's Background Information

The Republic of Gotonia covers an area of approximately 56,000 sq km. Its population, estimated at nearly 80 million in 1980, has been increasing at a rate of between 2.8 and 3 percent per annum. About one-tenth of its population lives in the urban areas. According to the official estimates, the gross domestic product of the country was estimated at US$8,800 million, and the per capita product at approximately US$110. Per capita gross domestic product is reported to have increased by about 1.4 percent annually between 1973 and 1980. Over 80 percent of the population have incomes below the amount that is needed to afford them two meals a day.

The economy is basically agricultural. Over half of the country's gross domestic product comes from agriculture, and only about 6 percent from modern industries. Nearly 26 percent is contributed by trade, transport, and services. Jute and tea are the main export commodities.

The main problems of the country can be traced back to (a) the neglect of agriculture in the sixties, which resulted in rapidly growing food imports; (b) polarized policies between regions and between rural and urban areas; and (c) adoption of a strategy that relied heavily on imported inputs and had very little domestic value-added content. The result is that the economic problems of Gotonia are dominated by a staggering balance of payments deficit, and an acute shortage of domestic resources. The country also has to look for new markets for its products. The situation was also made more difficult as the country had to face a massive task of rehabilitation and reconstruction of the economy.

The present government is conscious of the overwhelming problems of poverty, increasing income disparities, unemployment, illiteracy, high population growth rates, and slow pace of the growth of the economy. In its newly drafted second plan it has aimed its development objectives at:

1. acceleration of the pace of economic development
2. distribution of incomes, resources, and opportunities more equitably
3. improvement in the standard of living by ensuring adequate supplies of the basic needs
4. attainment of a higher degree of self-reliance

The government has strengthened its institutional framework for meeting the urgent needs of the economy. The roles of the various committees and authorities concerned with the implementation of various development programs have been clearly defined.

Socioeconomic Framework of the Project Area

The project area where IRDPGD will be taken up has a total area of 103 sq km. As mentioned above, its boundaries are coterminous with that of the Gotonia District, which borders Nagha to the west and north, and Goto to the east.* The existence of these foreign borders cannot be considered irrelevant to the country, and particularly this region's development. The capital of Gotonia District, that is, the project area, is 160 km. from the national capital.

The total population of the Gotonia District in 1981 was estimated at about 181,000, of which roughly 10 percent lived in urban areas. Average family size was 5.9 persons, having increased from 5.3 in 1961. Settlement is in the form of scattered compounds that combine to form loosely knit villages. Literacy rate is about 13 percent. There is no information on skill distribution of labor force. According to a recent survey, about 67 percent of the total population are cultivators, 16 percent are wage laborers, 7 percent are traders, and 10 percent are in public (including professional) services. Estimates of unemployment and underemployment are not available; it is generally believed that open unemployment in the District is negligible.

A recent study done by the Local Development Academy shows that 28.7 percent of the households in Gotonia District have an annual income of US$130 or more; 39.5 percent of the households reported their incomes ranging between $100 and $130, and the rest, 31.7 of the households, had incomes of less than $100. The Academy's survey results are consistent with the official estimates, although in the latter, the percentage of households in the over-$130 income category is somewhat higher.

Incidence of landlessness is higher in this District than the country as a whole. About 25 percent of the total households are landless, and another 30 percent functionally landless (having less than 0.2 hectare). The distribution of operational holdings is shown in Table 1.

Rainfall varies between 150 and 200 cm a year, of which 80 percent falls during the monsoon season, i.e., July to September. Agriculture is seriously hampered by lack of rainfall in other months. Torrential downpours occasionally cause flooding.

Soils in the project area are of alluvial origin, and form moderate to good agricultural lands. Although the natural fertility of soils is generally good, the soils along the rivers are lightly textured and cause high water losses, thus providing an impediment to the extension of

----

*It does not mean that the project will benefit the population of the entire District. An estimated 8,500 farm families are likely to benefit in the first instance.

TABLE 1
Size of operational holdings

Size in Hectares	% of Operational Holdings *
Upto 0.2 ha	13.60
0.2-0.4 ha	16.30
0.4-0.8 ha	25.40
0.8-2.02 ha	30.70
72.02	13.90
Total	100.00

*45 percent of households did not report any operating lands.

irrigated rice. Further, present farming operations are hampered by prevailing hydrological features--soils remain too wet in the monsoon period and too dry the rest of the year. The main source of irrigation in the project area is low-lift pumps, which are installed during the dry season near the banks of rivers.

Paddy is by far the most important crop in the project area. Other crops grown are jute, pulses, sugarcane, and oilseeds. In areas subject to flooding of 2 ft or over, farmers plant floating paddy. The area planted with floating paddy has been greatly reduced since the construction of a flood embankment. In areas free from frequent flooding, local paddy varieties are being replaced by high-yielding varieties (HYV).

Yields per hectare, generally low, vary considerably from year to year and even more so from farm to farm. Although covering only 12 percent of the cultivated area, HYV contribute nearly 20 percent of the total rice production; the potential yield of HYV is considerably higher than its present level.

Jute has long been the second most important crop, but it is gradually being substituted by food crops because of the increasing population and the unfavorable price for jute. Pulses and oilseeds currently rank second on the list of important crops. Yields of these crops are generally low, about 700-900 kg/ha, as very little fertilizer is applied and plants are grown on residual moisture during the dry season. Oilseeds are locally processed, leaving a high percentage of the oil in the cake.

The area under wheat has expanded in recent years. Local wheat varieties yielding about 900 kg/ha have been grown on a limited scale. High-yielding varieties of wheat have been introduced in recent years and the area with HYV wheat is expanding rapidly wherever means of irrigation are available.

The extent of irrigation by methods for 1981 is shown in Table 2. As would be seen, irrigation is almost entirely based on power pumps and tubewells. Canal irrigation is insignificant. Traditional methods such as doons or swing baskets have virtually disappeared.

Surveys show that there is considerable irrigation potential in the District that remains untapped. In two blocks of the District, the index of capacity utilization is 0.20 and 0.53; in the other two blocks, it is 0.70 and 0.83. The constraints on capacity utilization are both technical and socioeconomic. Technical factors include wrong siting of pumps, poor design of distributaries and conveyance systems resulting in large water losses and limited availability of water from natural sources. Socioeconomic factors include availability of supplies and services, prices of irrigation inputs, land fragmentation, and the size-tenure characteristics of farms in the District.

The research and farm extension services in the project area are inadequate. There is not a single research experiment station or demonstration farm. The main extension service is related to rice and wheat. The task of agricultural assistants--inadequate as they are in number--is multifarious, and very little time is devoted to providing technical services to the farmers. To strengthen the farm extension service, the government has decided to increase the number of assistants.

The major proportion of rural credit is provided by noninstitutional sources (e.g., money lenders, friends, or relatives). The main institutional sources of credit are

TABLE 2
Irrigation methods

Methods	Per cent
Power pumps	77.8
Tubewells	14.8
Doons	5.6
Canal	0.9
Others	0.9
Total	100.0
Irrigated area as % of net cropped area	9.01

the Gotonia Krishi Bank (GKB) and the Commercial Bank. GKB has extended primarily medium-term credit for bullocks, boats, and land development. The Commercial Bank has extended only short-term credit, and that, too, in a very limited total amount.

The health and family planning services are very poor. Approximately 50 percent of the population suffers from malnutrition, which is most severe with pre-school age children.

The Project

Objectives. The primary objective of the project is to improve agricultural productivity and living conditions of the rural people in the project area through a broad-based integrated development approach. The project seeks to provide a sustained growth in the economy of the area and stimulate participation of the rural population through revitalized cooperatives and improved and additional infrastructural and institutional facilities, aimed at increasing agricultural production, employment and income. The wider diffusion and sharing of employment and income opportunities would be sought through various integrated project activities and through a series of rural works programs.

Activities. The project has proposed the following main activities under its umbrella:

1. Infrastructure development consisting of (a) construction of flood embankments, (b) re-excavation of major drainage channels, (c) installation of tubewells, (d) improvement of existing unpaved roads.
2. Agriculture support facilities and services such as (a) the construction of rural markets, (b) a workshop for servicing deep tubewells and pumps, and (c) strengthening of cooperatives.
3. Community health programs and facilities for health and family planning.

Project costs and funding. The total capital costs of the project are estimated at US$600,000. A part of these costs may be mobilized externally. All operating costs will be borne by the Republic of Gotonia through resources raised locally.

Activity-wise capital costs are given in Table 3.

TABLE 3
Activity-wise capital costs

Category	Total Costs (US$)
Infrastructure development	220,000
Agriculture support facilities and services	310,000
Community health programme services	70,000
Total	600,000

Benefits and justification. The project would provide complete protection to the District from annual flooding, and would provide assured means of irrigation to nearly 50 percent of the cultivable lands. As a result, crop cultivation would be intensified and diversified. Paddy would continue to be the main crop during the wet season but traditional varieties would be replaced by high-yielding varieties. Wheat would become the second major crop and HYV wheat would be grown during the winter season. These two major crops would be supplemented by sugarcane, oilseeds, vegetables, and others. The farmers would be able to use higher levels of technical inputs, and these factors combined together would result in a sizeable increase in farm production in the project area.

Farm incomes. Irrigation, combined with flood protection and supplemented by an assured supply of farm inputs, improved extension services, more easily available credit, and better infrastructure, will lead to substantially improved incomes for farmers in the project area. Table 4 shows the expected increase in incomes of 8,500 farm families who are likely to derive direct benefits from the project. The costs and benefits of the IRDPGD are shown in Tables 5 through 7.

Integrated Approach to Development

By definition, an integrated area development means "an appropriate location of social and economic activities for balanced development over a physical space." The IRDPGD Project seems to meet the requirements of an integrated area development for the reasons stated below. The Gotonia Dis-

TABLE 4
Expected level of incomes from the project distributed by categories of farm families (in US$)

Category of Farm Families	Present Level of Income	% of the Average	Additional Income as a Result of the Project	Future Level of Incomes	% of the Average
Low-income farm families (5,000)	100	73	15	115	75
Average-income farm families (3,000)	180	131	18	198	129
High-income farm families (500)	250	182	20	270	176
Average	137		$16.3/ family	153	

trict development program is primarily concerned with the development of one of the republic's most backward areas. This program was mooted because past development planning and performance had led to regional imbalances in Gotonia with the District of Gotonia benefiting the least from the development efforts.

The project links an increment in GDP with rises in individual farmer income, improved communications, better nutrition and food storage for the participating families, increased popular participation in decision making at the local and intermediate level, and the build-up of new institutions and processes of development. The project is people-centered and regards the individual in the District as the agent, subject, and beneficiary of development.

The Integrated Development Programme for Gotonia District is thus meant to tackle the poverty and backwardness issues in the area by using the agricultural improvement scheme for the small farmer as the main thrust for raising farm family incomes, extending and improving the irrigation system; using agricultural extension services to propagate better farming methods, and providing, through the farm service centers, the facilities for processing, storing, and marketing the produce of small farmers, thereby bringing

TABLE 5
Items of costs and benefits of the IRDPGD (US$000)

Items	Years						
	0	1	2	3	4	5	6
A. Expected costs (Value of inputs)							
Capital	600	-	-	-	-	-	-
Operating							
Managerial/ technical services	50	50	55	57	57	57	57
Local labour	-	70	75	76	76	76	76
Rawmaterials (local)	-	70	75	78	80	80	80
Fuel	-	8.5	8.8	9	9.5	9.5	9.5
Services	-	7.5	7.5	7.5	7.5	7.5	7.5
Others	-	5.5	5.5	5.5	5.5	5.5	5.5
Interest on loans	-	30	30	30	30	30	30
Taxes	-	6	6	6	6	6	6
Depreciation	-	-	-	-	-	-	-
Sub-total	650	247.5	268.2	269	271.5	271.5	271.5
B. Expected benefits (Value of outputs)							
Sails	-	340	390	420	450	450	390
Subsidies	-	12	12	12	12	12	12
Value of assets at the end of the projects	-	-	-	-	-	-	60
Sub-total		352	402	432	462	462	462

TABLE 6
Costs and benefits of the IRDPGD (Financial) (US$000)

Year	Expected Costs (Outflows)			Expected Benefits (Inflows)	Benefits-Costs (Net Cash Flows)
	Capital	Operating Inc: Interest & Taxes	Total		
0	600	50	650		-650
1		247.5	247.5	352	104.5
2		262.8	262.8	402	139.2
3		269.0	269.0	432	163.0
4		271.5	271.5	462	190.5
5		271.5	271.5	462	190.5
6		271.5	271.5	422	150.5

Years	Values of Net Cash Flows at 10% Discount Rate		
	Discounted Value of 1	Net Cash Flows	Discounted Values
0	1	-650	-650
1	.909	104.5	95.0
2	.826	139.2	115.0
3	.751	163.0	122.4
4	.683	190.5	130.1
5	.621	190.5	118.3
6	.564	190.5	84.9
			665.7

Net Present Value: 665.7 - 650 = 15.7

IRR = 10.8

them into commercial agriculture. The build-up of extensive institutional support for the program described above ensures that the development scheme will give lasting benefit to the inhabitants of the District long after the project

TABLE 7
Costs and benefits of the IRDPGD (Economic) (US$000)

Year	Expected Costs (Outflows)			Expected Benefits (Inflows)	Benefits-Costs (Net Cash Flows)
	Capital	Operating Inc: Interest & Taxes	Total		
0	600	50	650	-	-650
1		206.5	206.5	340	133.5
2		219.3	219.3	390	170.7
3		224	224	420	196
4		225.5	225.5	450	224.5
5		225.5	225.5	450	224.5
6		225.5	225.5	450	224.5

Years	Values of Net Cash Flows at 15% Discount Rate		
	Discounted Value of 1	Net Cash Flows	Discounted Values
0	1	-650	-650
1	.869	133.5	116.0
2	.756	170.7	129.0
3	.657	196	128.8
4	.571	224.5	128.2
5	.497	224.5	111.6
6	.432	224.5	97.0
			710.6

Adjustments made:

Local labour at 50% of the market price

Net Present Value: 710.6 - 650 = 60.6

IRR = 17.8

period. To this extent the integrated approach to development analysis and planning is relevant to the development of Gotonia District.

Note: These sheets represent only a part of this folder.

6
Project Coordination for Local Development

What has so far been done in this volume is to demonstrate what planners need to know in order to identify and select local-level development projects. This volume has therefore addressed questions such as: What information should planners collect for this purpose? How should they scrutinize and analyze that information? In what way should they organize the results of the analysis? How should they read the results for purposes of decision making? While addressing these questions, the one stream of thought that flowed through this volume was that the project selection process is inextricably linked with, and not independent of, the overall goals of local development. The process of project selection is continuously guided, controlled, and facilitated by these goals, objectives, and sometimes even by development targets. The goals may be explicitly given, may be vague or implicit, but they are invariably in the forefront of project analysis. Losing sight of them means losing a sense of purpose and direction of development itself. Contrary to what many may believe, the project selection process is not benefit-cost analysis; rather, it is a process that involves examination of every single proposal with respect to local development goals and objectives.

When we view "project analysis" in this context, the question that arises is whether, as planners, we should limit our task to mere selection of individual development projects or, as argued in the initial chapter of this book, attempt to place these projects in a wider economic and social perspective, and thereby establish a better relationship between "projects" and "plans." As planners, should we consider our task complete the moment we have identified projects that we consider suitable, viable, and feasible, or should we extend the analysis to promote the idea of developing a "comprehensive planning methodology," and make planning a truly coordinated effort?

The situation existing in most developing countries is one in which there is no link between the selected projects and the local development plans. Sectoral functionaries identify and select development projects concerning their sectors, which usually include a wide assortment, e.g., road projects for villages A, B, C, and H; culvert projects for villages B and H; minor irrigation projects for villages A to H and M to Q; establishment of markets for villages A, B, and C; projects for the rehabilitation of derelict tanks in villages D, E, and F; school projects for villages A, D, G, and H; health center projects for villages M to Q; introduction of high-yielding varieties of maize projects in seven villages; and a score of others. Almost invariably, these functionaries consider their "planning tasks" to be complete the moment they have before them such sets of projects that may appear to them feasible and viable on financial, economic, and social grounds. The only other task that interests them at this stage is to somehow get the technical and related organizational details of such projects worked out so that they can be submitted for de jure approval and the necessary financial appropriations. They make no attempt to coordinate the projects; nor do thay make any assessment as to whether, cumulatively, these projects will bring about the kind of change they had envisaged prior to beginning the planning process.

The consequences of paying insufficient attention to "coordination" are known and fully documented. A large number of local areas and communities show clear signs of lopsided and unbalanced growth. There are numerous examples of unused services and facilities because of the absence of the necessary supportive projects. Problems of poverty, unemployment, and environmental degradation continue and even proliferate in spite of the projects, and can, to a very significant extent, be attributed to the absence of "coordination" as well as insufficient understanding in the countries of its objectives and operational mechanisms.

This volume takes the position that it is not sufficient for local-level planners to merely identify individual development projects and determine their relative feasibility. Of equal importance and necessity is project coordination. It is the premise here that if the aim of local level planning is balanced and harmonious development, then it is an essential requirement that projects be systematically coordinated.

Although the need for coordination is well entrenched

in planning sciences, attempts to define or even describe the term have been less successful.[1] Many planners dub this term as being one that is more easily understood than described. In the context of this book, the term "coordination" is used in the sense of a mechanism for bringing about compatibility, consistency, and harmony between different elements or stages of a planning exercise. The key issue regarding coordination, however, is not its definition, but what purposes can it serve, and in what manner can it strengthen the overall planning process. There are at least three purposes that coordination can serve, and that need to be noted by planners at local levels:

1. to bring about compatibility between the projects and local development plans
2. to enhance the overall development impact of projects by making them mutually supportive and complementary
3. to achieve balanced local development by a proper spatial distribution of projects

A brief explanation on each of the above purposes is considered useful.

One of the important purposes that can be served by coordination is to bring about overall consistency between "projects" and "plans," that is, between what benefits the projects cumulatively are expected to yield, and whether or not they are compatible with the development goals and objectives for the local area. The need for consistency between projects and plans has escalated in recent years, obviously on account of the widening discord between them. Considerable evidence has accumulated in the developing countries that show that the two exercises of "project selection" and plan-making are not only carried out in relative isolation, but rarely is any attempt made to link them, or coordinate them in order to see whether the two are moving toward or away from each other. One of the working papers prepared by the Iranian planning organization in 1975 observed in this regard that although the theoretical framework provided for a relationship between the macro and sectoral planning activities and project selection system, in practice the two bore no relationship at all.[2] There persists a wide gap between what the projects are intended to bring about and the framework of the plan. This may be seen in Figure 14.

Coordination is a device for eliminating the gap between projects and plans and for bringing about a greater

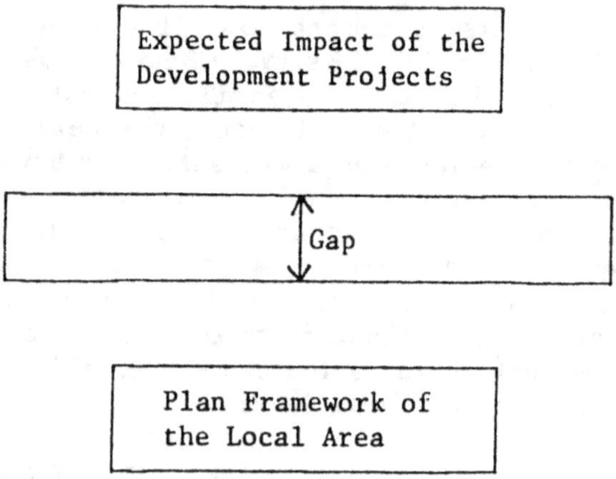

Figure 14. Gap between projects and the plan framework

degree of consistency between the two. It requires examining several interrelated questions such as: What will the projects cumulatively bring to the area? What pace and pattern of development will emerge if these projects are implemented? Will the pattern be in conformity with the local-level development plans? How large is the gap between the two, if any? What should be done to eliminate the gap? Would this require identification of new projects, reexamination of existing ones, or would it call for a reconsideration of the development plans? Stress is placed here on a qualitative assessment by planners in order to determine if the projects that they have identified would achieve the purposes and aims of local development.

A second objective underlying coordination is to identify gaps in linkages among projects, and to make them mutually supportive in order to enhance their overall development impact. Absence of linkages among projects has been observed as one of the major constraints to faster development at local levels. A project designed to increase maize production without simultaneously providing for a linked project that would economically utilize the increased maize production, or a health sector project for malaria control without linking it with water supply projects are examples of the absence of linkages among projects. Coordination helps in ascertaining whether or not such linked projects have been identified and provided for by the planners. It also helps in determining the nature of the projects--whether they are complementary, competitive, or substitutable.

Lastly, coordination is essential for achieving balanced spatial development. We often find that a primary school has been proposed for town A, while another nearby town has been selected for a health center, and a third town for the location of a cultural center. There are several instances where dairies have been established at one location while milk-processing plants are set up elsewhere. Lack of spatial coordination among projects reduces their overall effectiveness, and escalates development costs. Spatial coordination is a device that can increase projects' effectiveness and reduce development costs.

The approaches to project coordination at local levels depend on the number and kind of projects involved. In most cases, simple and straightforward approaches will be needed to achieve the above purposes. Only exceptionally, as in the case of projects with strong interdependencies, will more complicated methods of coordination be needed.

Projects are often interdependent through their inputs and outputs. Planners call such connections forward linkages (through outputs) and backward linkages (through inputs). If two projects are compared, one is able to immediately detect the existence or nonexistence of direct linkages. Where such linkages exist the scale of inputs and outputs must be additionally checked and coordinated.

More difficult is the coordination of projects where the interrelationship between them is only indirect, as for instance between a project aimed at increasing farm production and a project in the cultural sector, such as the establishment of a local library or cinema in the same area. The indirect link between such projects would have to be traced through, among other things, an increase in people's income what would result in more expenditure for cultural activities. The scope and strength of the indirect impact can sometimes be ascertained from past data from other areas.

If quantitative interrelationships among several projects involving the same product or service exist, a feasible way to make them consistent at the local and area levels would be through the preparation of a balance sheet. On one side all locally available quantities of the product or service can be listed, while on the other side all needed inputs, as expressed by the new projects as well as the existing facilities, could be stated. For instance, in respect of energy consumption, projects could be coordinated by drawing up a balance sheet that would, on one side, list all present and future demands for energy by existing industrial facilities, households, and the new projects, that can then be compared with the other side showing the available quantities of energy. Such a sheet would immediately show the balance between availability and requirements of energy. Similar balance sheets could be constructed for water, certain construction materials, or services needed by new investment projects.

Planning for local development is an intertwined and interactive exercise. Contrary to what many textbooks and guidelines suggest, this exercise is neither linear nor sequential. Indeed, all planning steps involved in the exercise act upon each other, and have, of necessity, to be coordinated successively in order to result in a plan that is internally consistent, and compatible with planners' visions or perceptions of local development.

If we view planning in this perspective, then it would be evident that the selection of development projects is a part of an overall development effort and not independent of it. Projects are not an end in themselves; rather, they are a means to attain specific development goals, objectives, and targets. Projects do not have any aims of their own. Individually, they may be feasible. They may show promise and potential. Systematic coordination, however, enhances their overall impact and leads to a balanced development of the area concerned.

NOTES

1. Masahiko Honjo, "Implementing the Development Plans: Focus on Coordination," in R. P. Misra and Masahiko Honjo, eds., Changing Perception of Development Problems, Regional Development Series Volume 1, United Nations Centre for Regional Development (Singapore: Maruzen Asia, 1981).

2. Plan and Budget Organization, "Towards Preparation of the Sixth Development Plan: A Proposed Planning System for Iran," Tehran, December 1975.

References for Advanced Reading

CHAPTER 1

Chambers, Robert, Rural Development: Putting the Last First (London: Longman, 1983).

Dias, Hiran D., and B.W.E. Wickramanayake, Manual for Training in Rural Development Planning (Bangkok: Human Settlement Division, Asian Institute of Technology, 1983).

Hirschman, Albert O., Development Projects Observed (Washington, D.C.: The Brookings Institute, 1967).

United Nations, Economic and Social Commission for Asia and the Pacific, Guidelines for Rural Centre Planning (New York: United Nations, 1979).

Watertson, Albert, Developing Planning: Lessons of Experience, A World Bank Publication, published for the Economic Development Institute of the World Bank (Baltimore and London: The Johns Hopkins University Press, 1965).

CHAPTER 2

Cochrane, Glenn, The Cultural Appraisal of Development Projects (New York: Praeger Publishers, 1979).

Harper, Malcolm, and Tan Thiam Soon, Small Enterprises in Developing Countries (London: Intermediate Technology Publications Ltd., 1979).

Lapin, Lawrence, Statistics: Meaning and Method, second edition (New York: Harcourt Brace Jovanovich, Inc., 1980).

Sen, Amartya, Employment, Technology, and Development (Oxford: Clarendon Press, 1975).

Singer, Hans, Technologies for Basic Needs (Geneva: International Labour Office, 1977).

Smith, David M., Industrial Location (New York and London: John Wiley & Sons, Inc., 1971).

White, Lawrence J., "Appropriate Factor Proportions for Manufacturing in Less Developing Countries: A Survey of the Evidence" (Princeton, N.J.: Woodrow Wilson School of Public and International Affairs, Princeton University).

CHAPTER 3

Cairncross, Sandy, Jan Carruthers, Donald Curtis, Richard Feachem, David Bradley, and George Baldwin, Evaluation for Village Water Supply Planning, published in association with International Reference Center for Community Water Supply (New York and London: John Wiley & Sons, Inc., 1980).

Gittinger, J. Price, Economic Analysis of Agricultural Projects, EDI Series in Economic Development, published for the Economic Development Institute of the World Bank (Baltimore and London: The Johns Hopkins Press, 1982).

Little, J.M.D., and J. A. Mirrlees, Project Appraisal and Planning for Developing Countries (London: Heinamann Educational Books, 1974).

Prest, A. R., and R. Turvey, "Cost-Benefit Analysis: A Survey," Economic Journal (New York: Cambridge University Press, December 1965).

Squire, Lyn, and Herman G. van der Tak, Economic Analysis of Projects, A World Bank Research Publication (Baltimore and London: The Johns Hopkins University Press, 1976).

United Nations Industrial Development Organization, Guidelines for Project Evaluation (New York: United Nations, 1972).

United Nations Industrial Development Organization, Manual for the Preparation of Industrial Feasibility Studies (New York: United Nations, 1978).

CHAPTER 4

Hill, Morris, Planning for Multiple Objectives, Monograph Series No. 5 (Philadelphia: Regional Science Research Institute, 1973).

MacArthur, J. D., and Galal A. Amin (eds.), World Development, Vol. 6, No. 2 (Oxford and New York: Pergamon Press Ltd., 1978).

Ray, Anandarup, and Herman G. van der Tak, "A New Approach to the Economic Analysis of Projects," Finance and Development, Vol. 16, No.1 (March 1979).

Schwefel, Detlef, "Who Benefits from Production and Employment?--Six Criteria to Measure the Impact of Development Projects on Poverty and Satisfaction of Basic Needs" (monograph) (Berlin: German Development Institute, 1975).

University of Sussex, IDS Bulletin, Vol. 10, No. 1 (Brighton: Institute of Development Studies, University of Sussex, August 1978).

CHAPTER 5

Roemer, Michael, and Joseph J. Stern, The Appraisal of Development Projects: A Practical Guide to Project Analysis with Case Studies and Solutions (New York: Praeger Publishers, 1975).

CHAPTER 6

Little, I.M.D., and J. A. Mirrlees, Project Appraisal and Planning for Developing Countries (London: Heinemann Educational Books, 1974).

United Nations Economic and Social Commission for Asia and the Pacific, Guidelines for Rural Centre Planning (New York: United Nations, 1979).

Index

For Product Safety Concerns and Information please contact our EU representative GPSR@taylorandfrancis.com
Taylor & Francis Verlag GmbH, Kaufingerstraße 24, 80331 München, Germany

www.ingramcontent.com/pod-product-compliance
Lightning Source LLC
LaVergne TN
LVHW021621091026
849796LV00027B/353
9780367299903